Africa and the Cities of Stone

Africa and the Cities of Stone

* * *

Eric P. Mitchell

ISBN-13: 9781537375977
ISBN-10: 1537375970
Library of Congress Control Number: 2016916025
CreateSpace Independent Publishing Platform
North Charleston, South Carolina

Acknowledgements

Thanks to Mom and Dad for the assist in Zimbabwe.

Special Thanks to Gary Himes and Noelle K. Sereda for the proofreading.

Contents

List of Pictures

Introduction: Winter 2013

I'd had enough of my job! The last few years had been spent playing the role of corporate IT analyst on a helpdesk wasteland in Northern Kentucky; a daily grind of password resets, system reboots, software installations, and profile setups over-and-over-and-over. Occasionally, the work was interesting, but mostly it was like shoveling coal; everyday there was a new pile to move. Fortunately, I worked second shift. So, as the demands of the business day tapered off and the call volume dissipated, there was an hour or two of free time every night. It was spent reconnoitering the African continent via Google Earth.

I'd traveled to Africa before (and I wanted to return). Previous excursions to both Kenya and Ghana had yielded magazine articles on lost cities and forgotten treasure. This time, I wanted to accomplish something much bigger and more in depth. So, while scanning the shore lines, river basins and built up areas I began to plot a route of travel. The trip would begin in the highlands of Ethiopia, skirt the coast along the Indian Ocean, penetrate the interior and then culminate in the grassy region of South Africa known as the Veldt. There'd be stops along the way too- visits to ancient ruins built from the three rock types- sedimentary, metamorphic and igneous.

There'd be no safari vans, no fancy hotels, plush bedding or fresh towels. I'd be grinding it out in the streets (the best way to experience the Motherland), eating at little chop joints and bunking down at the corner guest house for twenty bucks a night. Point A-to-B would be covered by local transport, where I would meet scores of people and see fascinating landscapes, both urban and rural. Best of all, I'd be examining archaeology with pen and paper in hand (a hobby of mine).

Despite shaving the edges on expenditures (I'd packed my lunch every day for years) the trip would be tight financially. I might even break the bank, but who cared? It was time to cut out! Right when I had enough money saved up, I handed the boss my notice. Two weeks later, I signed off for the last time and then the next day, hopped a flight to the Horn of Africa, beginning my tour of the cities of stone.

Ethiopia: the Beginning

I

Axum

Look at a map of East Africa and you'll find the city of Axum saddled down in Tigray, an arid and rugged province in Ethiopia's northern frontier. It's just there, northwest of the Horn. In the distant past, Axum was the capital of an empire founded sometime between 150 BC and 50 AD. As the seat of government, Axum's authority spanned a region that centered on modern day northern Ethiopia and southern Eritrea. At times, its sphere of influence straddled the Nile river and reached across the Red Sea, jabbing into the under belly of the Arabian Peninsula. The cities and towns of this ancient empire are silted over with dirt, stones and other debris, but archaeologists have managed to uncover a number of sites.

At the height of its glory, Axum issued its own coinage; gold for international transactions while silver and copper circulated amongst the general population. From Adulis, her Red Sea port, Axumite traders worked deals with Egyptian, Roman, Indian and Sri Lankan merchants. Large quantities of natural resources (gold, ivory and incense) were exchanged for metal works, weapons, fabrics, wines and olive oil.

Early on, the Axumites followed an ancient religion that originated in Southern Arabia, but in the fourth century AD the state religion shifted to Christianity. With the coming of Islam, the trading routes were choked off and Axum was reduced to a forgotten backwater. For centuries the place lay dormant and Arab chroniclers recorded fighting among the population.

In the late 1880's, renowned Victorian traveler J. Theodore Bent noted the solid nature of the local housing, but wrote about the difficulty securing acceptable accommodations. Once settled in, his observations included food shortages at the market, a peculiar arrangement where criminals of all kinds found refuge without fear of arrest and scores of people with ghastly afflictions like leprosy and elephantiasis.

Upon arrival in Axum, I'd booked a 200 Birr room at the Abinet Hotel. This place was a special case. All the wood furnishings were dented, chipped or splintered. Someone had ripped the door off the closet cabinet and left it for dead on the top shelf. The bed sagged miserably in the middle. The fixtures on the bathroom sink wobbled like drunken belly dancers and the lid to the toilet reservoir was gone. Flushing was accomplished by prodding a piece of plastic mounted dead center at water level of the tank, but this had complications. At the slightest infraction the plastic tube dislodged and bobbed about like debris on the high seas, preventing the reservoir from replenishing. However, the lavatory did have a locking door and key. So, I secured my gear to the sink drainage pipe with a bike cable and a Masters combination lock before locking it down a second time.

Don't get me wrong, the Abinet wasn't all bad. There were a couple of bright spots: first, the hotel had its own restaurant. The locals packed the joint and shoveled down platefuls of spicy food and their bread, injera (a thin spongy pancake that is sour to the taste). A couple of times, I joined in and crushed a serving of Doro Wat, spicy tomato stew stocked with any parts chicken and one egg. The sauce is poured over injera or regular bread, but no matter how often I asked for it with rice, the waitress refused. Breakfast was a meat omelet washed down by a cup of hot tea. Second, the room came with a small balcony that overlooked a four lane boulevard divided by a median of palm trees. Blue and white tuk-tuks (motorized rickshaws) whizzed by alone or in formation. After a gap, traffic would resume in the form of a truck, car, mini-bus or bicyclist riding against oncoming traffic.

Street side was a mix of grocery stores, butcher shops, clothing stores, coffee houses and cafes. Loud-but-inviting Ethiopian Jazz music emanated from drinking spots and eateries. Skinny people in baggy clothes drifted along either side of the road. They were a dusty brown complexion, but some a few shades darker. The overwhelming majority had sharp facial features, like Arabs. Every so often a face in the crowd resembled someone from Southern India or Sri Lanka. Tigray women (Tigray people are the dominant ethnic group in the north) had crosses or sun symbols tattooed on their foreheads and temples. Bushy haired lads who looked like they'd just hiked in from the Danikal, a nasty desert to the east, crowded the corners.

Being that I'm going to quote everything in Ethiopian currency, I'll give you the low down on their monetary system. At the time of travel the exchange rate was 18.24 Birr for one US Dollar. You could buy a 350 ml bottle of Coca-Cola for between 6-15 Birr. Fifty percent of the currency in circulation was soiled so heavily it looked like a layer of fungus had taken root. These bills showed all the indications of enduring a suffocating life tucked away in someone's dark moist spot. After touching these little rags you'll get an urge to wash your hands like you've never had before.

Word on the street, at the time of my visit, was that UNESCO was buying up big chunks of real estate because whenever the natives dug out a basement they hit a tomb or some kind of artifact. This is what makes Axum so great: the archeology. Megalithic tombs, fantastic obelisks, colossal thrones and the remains of other stone works are scattered around everywhere. Axum even has its own version of the Rosetta Stone. Known as the Ezana stone, this slab of rock is inscribed with three different languages that document the military adventures of an ancient king. Greek text is on one side and the opposite is covered in Ge'ez and Epigraphic South Arabian. However, the most intriguing aspect of Axum's archaeological history is what lies hidden away within Mayam Seyon church: Ethiopians claim it holds the Ark of the Covenant.

Eager to see some ruins, I started the first morning by flagging down a tuk-tuk and organizing a ride. Before we get going, there's something you need to know. Everywhere in the world, drivers prey on tourists and travelers. They think nothing of soaking some dummy for as much dough as possible. So, when you start negotiating a fare, slide on your brass knuckles and beat these guys down (figuratively, that is). This may sound a bit coarse, but failing to maintain the proper attitude can result in serious financial injury.

"How much to the Gudit Stelae Field?" I asked the driver of a beat up Tuk-Tuk. Gudit, just west of Axum, was my first stop. Stelae are massive stone slabs that have been positioned to stand upright.

"I don't know the place," he responded.

"What!" I said, and then waved him off.

A few minutes later, another tuk-tuk pulled over. "I need to get to Gudit Stelae Field, buddy."

"Fifty Birr for you, my friend," the driver smiled.

"How about ten?" I countered, having scooped the local price from the front desk clerk at my hotel.

"The cost is fifty," he stated firmly.

"Fat chance, buddy," I responded, and then signaled a third ride.

"Ok, ok!" He grumbled, and opened the side door on his tiny vehicle. Hurriedly, I squeezed into the confines of the back seat, clipping my knee caps in the process.

"Away!" I shouted.

Since the driver had a bit ground to cover, let's grab a refresher in geology 101 and cover the three types of rock: igneous, sedimentary and metamorphic.

Molten lava that cools above the ground or below the earth's surface is known as igneous rock. This is one of the two hard-rock types, meaning their consistency is very dense and heavy. Basalt, granite and pumice are examples of this type of rock. Particles of pre-existing rocks and dissolved materials accumulate to form sedimentary rocks. This is a soft rock and easily identified by viewing the layers in a cross section of a sample. It also holds fossils. Shale, limestone and sandstone are examples. Pre-existing rocks that undergo change by heat and pressure are called metamorphic. Quartzite, slate and marble are examples of this type, the other hard-rock.

After a bit of wandering we arrived at Gudit's main gate. Upon jumping out of the vehicle, I was set up by downtrodden youth pushing fake Axumite coins and fractured geodes- hollow spherical rocks that are lined with crystals.

"Sir, can I show you something?" they yelled in unison.

"No!" I answered, and kept on target for the entrance.

"Mister, I like your pen," one of them said, hoping to score a freebie.

"I like it more!" I bellowed, and the pack broke ranks wide enough so I could enter the site unhindered.

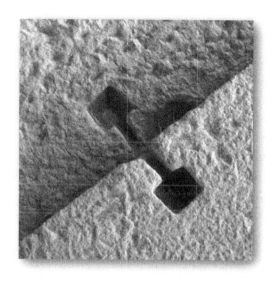

II

Of Tombs and Stelae

Cattle, donkeys and sheep grazed lazily amongst the stone garden while the sound of automatic gunfire rattled off in the distance (the police maintained a range nearby). It is said the name Gudit comes from a queen who conquered Axum in 980 AD. Through the years, the number of stelae has varied. In 1841, a Frenchman called Lefebvre tallied 52 stones. A German expedition logged 44 in 1906. Personally, I didn't bother with a head count. Rather, I just drifted across the grounds and began to speculate on their origins.

Most of the stelae still standing are unrefined rock listing precariously to one side. The stones bear no resemblance to the sophisticated culture Axum is known for. Instead, they look like they'd been pried away from a volcanic plug and then heaved into place by hairy brutes wearing animal skins. Now I'm not trying to take anything away from these prehistoric workings, because getting these rocks into position surely took planning, allocating resources and organizing a labor pool. Perhaps they could be the first endeavors of cavemen who thought beyond the necessities of life; raising crude monoliths in tribute to fallen warriors or philosophical wonderings.

Lying amongst the shanks of rock were a handful of real monoliths, granite that had been worked into a general shape; a solid base tapering up to a rounded top. With exception to the cross hatch pattern engraved in the rocks surface during the filing down process, there are no finishing details.

Across the road is another site referred to as Sheba's or Dungur Palace. Somehow, the ruins have been linked to the historical figure, the Queen of Sheba, probably to make a buck. However, I was informed by an unsanctioned guide, the place was a collection point for the Tax Man. The duty was paid in grain or other agricultural products. It makes sense, because if you look at an overhead shot of the place, it's made up of dozens of small rooms where you can stash lots of stuff.

A big wall marks the perimeter. Inside, the caretaker, a mid-aged man with a scruffy beard, followed along and mumbled something about "the ovens". Rats darted in and out of gaps between the stones. After a quick walk through the maze of compartments,

I made a final appraisal from the small observation deck at the rear of the site.

The vast majority of the structure was stacked up from tons of rocks fitted intricately together in a three tier design (the stones look like they were dug out of a field). But this work is completely overshadowed by much larger blocks fitted into the construction. The highest concentration of theses old stones is in the central walls, but there were other fixtures worked in too. In parts of the site, circular cut and angled stone have been set in as flooring. There are also drainage pieces built into the walls and whole sections of stairs incorporated into the layout.

Again, not to take anything away from the builders, but the rectangular blocks are formidable when compared to the much smaller and unrefined field rock. Possibly they reflect the work of a more advanced culture dating further back in antiquity. After being disassembled they were used by a less developed society (we'll be seeing more of this). The original builders were then reduced to a fleeting memory or myth when their architectural efforts were recycled into inferior grade buildings.

Rounding up another tuk-tuk, I headed to Axum's main attraction, the Stelae Park. Before entering the grounds, I was waved down by a gaunt figure dressed in tired clothing.

"Can you visit my shop?" he asked slowly, and then pointed to a chipped wooden door. "It's just here."

Venturing inside, I'd expected to find the normal assembly of dusty clothes, faded paintings and weathered post cards. However, the dingy compartment held a single frame bed, a battered wooden table and a TV set covered with industrial grade plastic. Three shelves spanned the back wall. An assortment of small metal objects and ornate metal crosses were deposited on each level. In the corner of the room, a small cooker, a handful of molds and a set of blackened utensils were piled up on the floor.

Like all curio dealers, the owner pushed his wares, but I wasn't buying. I never buy, because carrying all that stuff around just slows you down. Prior to exiting his room, I glanced at a portrait of a man and beautiful woman mounted on the wall.

"Is that Haile Selaisse?" I asked. Selaisse was Emperor of Ethiopia from 1930 until being ousted by a military committee in 1974.

"No," he corrected me. "That is my wedding day."

Upon closer inspection, it was him. The couple's stately posture and crisp white clothing suggested a more affluent life in the man's past. Somehow he'd been reduced to this grubby hole, eking out a life on the curio circuit. That's Africa for you. Fortunes come and go at the blink of an eye. One day you're a big man and the next, on the corner peddling for a bottle of beer.

The park's focal point is three massive granite obelisks referred to as the Royal Stelae. Traits of the Axumite style are repetitive geometric features, false doors and windows carved into the granite. From afar, they are like beacons to a civilization lost in the mists of time. Up close, they are absolutely fantastic.

By far the most impressive of the lot is the Great Stelae, despite being toppled centuries ago. In its original form archaeologists estimate that it stood nearly 33 meters tall and weighed 500 plus tons; its size and immensity eclipsed only by the mammoth works at Baalbek, Lebanon (those blocks weight between

750-1,000 tons). These days, it lies fragmented across the ground like a slain beast; either the victim of vandals, seismic activity or unclear engineering techniques.

Next in line is the Axum Obelisk. It comes in at 24 meters high. This piece, as well, was toppled some time ago. However, the pieces were salvaged by the Italian Army back in 1935 and then shipped to Rome for renovation. Reassembled in a small park, the trophy stood tall in the Italian capital for nearly seventy years, symbolic of Italy's African campaign. Finally, after much controversy, it was taken down, boxed up and then flown back to Ethiopia. In 2008 the stelae was reset in Axum. Today, it is the most eye catching of all, because having been put back into place with the most modern technologies, it stands like a sentinel, upright and straight.

At 21 meters high, King Ezana's Stelae is the smallest of the trio. However, its track record for endurance is solid. Through the years, travelers have noted it as the survivor, though it isn't impervious to age. These days, two massive counter weights are situated on either side to stabilize the tilting obelisk.

The balance, artistry and grandeur of these megalithic sculptures is very impressive, but ask yourself, does their power come in the form of a perfectly balanced megalithic stone, or, in wondering how much damage it will do when falling down? Let's reminisce on the Great Stelae for a moment.

Even in its derelict state, this thing is still a beast and its strength measured by the destruction of the tomb it landed on. If still erect, would it be seen as an object of admiration or worship as now? That said, I returned my gaze upon the King Ezana

Stelae and pondered watching it crash into the parking lot and reduce a tour bus to a crushed beer can. Talk about an object lesson in force and magnitude!

Beyond the show pieces, there are more stelae scattered about the grounds. They come in many shapes and conditions. Most are tall, needle-like and have angled tops. Some are half buried or sunken into the soil. They lack the details of their Axumite brethren, but their monolithic form is still thought provoking.

The Stelae Park is home to a handful of tombs too. Situated in the western corner of the park is the Tomb of the False Door. It's named after a massive block with a doorway carved on its façade: the false door. Above ground, stacks of large rectangular blocks lay about in a state of dishevelment. Adjoining stones along the foundation share perpendicular cutouts shaped like ties and filled in with metal. They look like giant staples or brackets employed to keep the stones in alignment (similar implements can be found in the ruins at Tiahuanaco, Bolivia). Inside the tomb itself, the quality of workmanship is superb; the stones are true and the joints tightly fitted.

Nearby the chips and chunks of the Great Stelae is a ten chamber tomb called the Mausoleum. Excavations were carried out in the past, but few artifacts were uncovered. There is also the Tomb of the Brick Arches, distinguished by a long staircase that plunges down to a horse shoe-shaped brick archway that leads to four rock-cut chambers. Despite being ransacked by grave robbers, archeologists recovered trace amounts of gold, silver and bronze objects.

However, the most impressive tomb is Nefas Mwacha. Locals call it Emmi Admas, a term that refers to the technology used to quarry Axum's massive stone works by the ancients. Imagine a machine that could manipulate solid matter at the atomic level by way of a beam of sound: mold, shape, hew or cut rock at perfect angles. If that beam could be adjusted to different frequencies, it might cause very heavy objects to vibrate in such a manner they became weightless. To this day it is thought to still be buried in the rubble.

The adjoining stelae field should be called the battlefield. With exception to the cave man delights, every stelae has been waylaid; knocked to the ground and the fragments embedded in the soil. Amongst the slaughter, there are some very nice specimens with interesting designs. One has a house on both sides of the stone; it's said to represent the Ark of the Covenant. Several are in the Axum style and there is one with several rows of dots rising along at an angle. Other stelae have their own unique sets of notches or repetitive designs.

There is another site further beyond the last stelae field called King Kaleb's Tombs. Kaleb was a sixth century king of Axum. An unpaved road covered with industrial grade gravel leads the way uphill. Travel books claim it's only a couple miles hike, but if you're humping a backpack full of sensitive items (like me), it will seem like a five mile slog. Stay alert for any bulls heading back down into town. They have a tendency to stop and snort loudly. When they dip their head and rake the ground with a front hoof, bolt towards the side of the road. You can take a defensive position behind the stone wall that runs parallel with the shoulder.

Above ground the structures are identical to the Queen of Sheba Palace. Thousands of rocks are fitted together in multitiered walls and massive blocks are stacked along the corners, worked into the walls and used for steps. The blocks set as corner pieces have notches cut into the edges facing inwards. Now, I'm not an archaeologist or a structural engineer, but on face value I think it is clear: the large refined gray stones are the remains of an interlocking system of masonry. The two tombs are accessed by descending a flight of steps into dank and dimly lit chambers. Each is sub-divided into multiple rooms. Both are rumored to have been loaded with vast quantities of treasure.

The masonry inside King Kaleb's Tomb is like a jigsaw puzzle. Although loose (possibly due to tectonic action), stones of all sizes have been cut into polygonal shapes and then fitted together. The face of each one is roughly hewn. One of the largest has eleven different angles, very similar to the Inca sites in South America. A smaller one is cut almost to a perfect triangle.

Masonry like this is found all over the world. In a YouTube video called "The Lost Cities of Ancient Worlds" rogue archaeologist David Hatcher Childress discusses "Cyclopean Masonry". At the 6:40 mark of the presentation, he provides three examples of the "jigsaw style"; the ancient city of Cusco in Peru, the Emperor's Palace in Tokyo Japan, and a site called the Necromanteion in Greece. Check it out online for yourself. In each example, newer structures sit on top of much older masonry, but these aren't the only examples. Conducting a brief Internet reconnaissance, I found another site with just a few mouse clicks. In the Peloponnese region of Greece, there is a place called Agio Adrianos Katsingri or Nafplio Af. Adrianos. From what few pictures are available, you can see a structure built from polygonal rocks with an interesting entrance that tapers in at the top; very similar to the doorways at Machu Picchu in South America.

The second tomb is called Gabra Masqal, named after Kaleb's son. It is constructed from stout rectangular blocks almost identical to the Tomb of the False Door. However, these stones interlock. In some instances, a gap has been left in the masonry and then filled in with a much smaller block; like a keystone. Three stone sarcophagi have been deposited in one of the rooms, but who's to say they weren't dragged into the "tomb" centuries if not millennia after its initial construction?

Now that we've seen a few styles of masonry, we should catch up on the work of Harry Thurston Peck. He was a classical scholar during the early 1900's who divided Cyclopean masonry into four styles: unwrought stones of various sizes, polygonal stones precisely interlocked together, stone course of the same height but unequal size, and horizontal courses of rectangular masonry of differing height.

Finding refuge in a shady spot, I began to ponder the similarities found in Axum with other sites around the world. When considering such a building technique, two theories of origin are up for deliberation. First, is it possible there was a school of masonry in a central location that students from all over the world attended? Or, secondly, could an advanced civilization have built outposts around the globe thousands of years ago? If so, who were they and why did they do it? Despite being called tombs and palaces, it might be possible the initial constructions were vaults or time capsules. In regards to the builders, the automatic response is Axumites or Sabaens. However, could it have been an ancient race yet to be fully recognized by conventional archaeologists?

III

The Valley of the Gods

After a day's rest, I was back on the trail, this time visiting a mysterious temple further to the north. An unofficial guide (more on him later) helped setup this excursion. The driver, Henok, was class-A. Once at the objective, he gunned it through Yeha village, clipping a goat and overrunning some chickens before skidding into the car park. This might sound intense, but it was nothing. When a pack of feral children threw rocks at his Toyota Four-Runner, he braked abruptly, jumped out, and then returned fire until they retreated from the roadside.

Before the dust had settled, I was out of the vehicle and charging up the fortified hill in front of us; just footsteps away from imbibing the historic splendor of a structure thousands of years old. Upon crashing the gate, my jaw dropped in disbelief; all the excitement accumulated during the ride up collapsed faster than a blazing dirigible. As adventurers, we want ruins half buried in the sand, on the verge of being swallowed up by the sea, or cloaked in layers of jungle foliage. But caged up in a mesh of metallic scaffolding the temple resembled an X-ray telescope more than the architectural icon of a lost civilization. Dashed, dismayed and disappointed, I staggered into the confines of the stone structure, sat down on a large block and collected my thoughts.

Yeha Temple, The Temple of the Moon, or Al Moqwa (as it is sometimes known) stands fifty feet high, forty-nine feet wide and sixty-one feet long. Yellowish in color, the building is constructed of fifty-two courses of finely cut and mortarless sandstone masonry. Long and short blocks interlock to form an inner and outer wall. These stones have been assembled so tightly you cannot insert a coin, knife or any other instrument into the joints. Square holes have been cut into the interior walls. Large square foot stones for support pillars are still in place at intervals along the flooring. Because of these features, it has been theorized that the structure was initially two levels. Through time, though, a considerable number of stones have been removed from the building. Despite being Ethiopia's oldest standing structure the state of preservation is considered remarkable for its age. This is attributed to the site being converted to a Christian church in the 6th century.

Listening to the resonance of village life play out below and the visceral cry of a strange looking bird overhead, I began to see past the metal grating and ponder the known history of this temple. It has been written that Yeha Temple was part of Di'amat, a kingdom founded over two thousand years ago by Sabaeans from Southern Arabia (now known as Yemen). These colonists are thought to have built the ancient ruins that dot modern day Eritrea and Ethiopia.

Through the centuries Yeha Temple has been visited by a handful of European explorers. Francisco Alvares, the Portuguese adventurer, came to the site in the 16th century and christened the temple "Abafacem". Another Portuguese, Jesuit Father Manuel Barradas, visited in 1634 and referred to the structure as unfinished, overgrown with vegetation and home to all things wild. Almost two hundred years later in 1810, Henry Salt, the British artist, discovered stone fragments with various inscriptions. He was informed by the local inhabitants that the Ark of the Covenant had been stashed away within the temple walls for some time.

Our friend Theodore Bent visited the temple for two days in 1893 and chronicled the experience in his book "The Sacred City of the Ethiopians". After surveying the ruins, he accurately proclaimed the temple as "a massive piece of masonry". He also wrote "my impression is strongly in favor of this building having been a temple dedicated to the old Sabaean cult of the sun and star worship". Bent also surmised that "the Yeha ruins are undoubtedly on the ancient road between Adulis and Aksum" (the former is a historic site on the Red Sea in Eritrea). Other visitors in the late 19th century described the interior as being filled with rubble and debris.

Through the 20th century a number of excavations have been carried out on the site. In 1906, the Deutsch Aksum-Expedition(DAE) conducted photographic documentation of the temple and pre-pared plans of its layout. Team members also recovered glass frag-ments and bronze lamps dated to the 6th century. Work completed by Jean Doresse in 1955 revealed a circular baptistery almost four feet deep. It contained two sets of stairs facing each other on an east-west axis. Other digs revealed graves in the hillside below the temple. The contents included skeletons, vessels of pottery, stone incense burners, bronze animals marked with south Arabian letters and a wide range of metal implements.

Gazing up at the highest reaches of the interior, I pondered the faces and voices this structure had witnessed through the centuries. Who built this place and why? What tools or school of mathematics had been employed to fabricate such precise masonry? Had there been human sacrifice or grand ceremonies lasting into the night? Imagine, the smoke from burning incense churning through the nocturnal air, fires alight and shadows dancing across the stone walls, chanting priests, and a hooded overlord with a bejeweled staff awaiting a celestial arrival.

With interests rekindled, I strolled along the outer wall of the temple. It's a stout stone rectangle, solid, yet victim to the work of Mother Nature. In certain sections, the stone is cracking and flaking away. Other parts show the wear of running water. On the inside, the interior walls are missing higher up and sections of the flooring have been stripped away. Outside, small planks of stone set vertically into the ground mark a cemetery that encircles the temple. Two crudely shaped monoliths are situated either side of the entrance, but the quality of workmanship does not match the temple masonry, suggesting a different effort all together.

Nearby, there is the Abba Afse church and a small building called the Treasury. Turbaned priests can be seen at both, but the Treasury also has a small museum on the second floor. Up top, there is a collection of crowns, 800 year old books, and paintings of St. George slaying the dragon. However, the most fascinating artifacts are the stone blocks engraved with Sabaean script. One even shows the divine symbol of southern Arabia- a disc and a crescent.

Through the years, travelers have reported the most detailed masonry being incorporated into nearby buildings. High up on the façade of Abba Afse you can see a stone block with a row of carved ibex heads.

Tracings of specimens showing Sabaean script were collected by Bent and then presented to Dr. David Heinrich Muller, a University of Vienna professor, for translation. Under careful scrutiny, Muller was able to identify the following references "he went into the valley", "under the protection of the deity" and "he built his house A.W.M.". Through these initials Muller saw a link to the word Ava, which Bent speculated was the temple's original name.

And so the afternoon went, lap-after-lap, rounding the four corners of the temple and then landing on that same foot stone that pulled me in the first time. Good or bad, I began to wonder if there were any consequences to such repetitive behavior; could such action spawn a winged serpent or would they reveal a beautiful maiden in search of carnal pleasures.

On the final lap, I shifted my gaze onto the surrounding landscape. Yeha Temple lies in a narrow valley. The Adwa Mountains are nearby, a formation of phono-lite plugs and domes (the solidi-fied cores of eroded volcanoes) overlooking the nearby hills. They are a testimony to the age of our beautiful Earth, but instead of symbolizing a past geologic era, they exude the metaphysical presence of planetary elders or ancestral spirits watching over and preserving this magnificent stone temple.

IV

Code Name: Gelila

A few hours later I'd come down from that temple high and caught up with my Axumite guide at one of the side walk cafes. Due to the sensitivity of the next operation and possible legal repercussions from the Ethiopian Antiquities Commission; I can only refer to him as Gelila. Perpetually gripped by consternation, he wasn't quite African or Arab, but somewhere in the middle.

Over a couple of rounds of drink, I told Gelila how much I enjoyed Yeha Temple and then forked over payment. Soon after, he got to squawking about another set of ruins.

"Eric!" he raved. "There is virgin site. Only a few people know about it."

"Where at?" I asked, as the excitement of visiting unknown ruins began to surge through my body.

"It's only twenty-seven kilometers by transport. From there we walk, but just short distance."

This sounded great and Gelila had delivered on Yeha Temple, but I needed to clarify this wouldn't devolve into an Ethiopian Snipe Hunt. "What will we find?"

"Big blocks, Eric," Gelila said, and then shook his hands vigorously like he was clutching a heavy stone. "But they have all fallen down. It's a very old temple, maybe even before Christ."

"Big blocks, eh?" I echoed, imagining the collapsed remains of a megalithic temple tucked away in the nooks and crannies of Northern Ethiopia. "How much?"

"For this one 600 Birr," he stated.

"Let's try 300," I countered, cutting his offer in half.

"It's only 35 Dollars, Eric," he pleaded. "That is fair price."

Thirty-five bucks didn't seem like much, but I was on budget and had to shave the edges at all times. So, I made my last offer. "I got three ten dollar bills, pal!"

"No problem," he replied. "Tomorrow we go."

And we did; rallying up at 2:30 in the afternoon, Gelila and I made our way to the bus station. After standing around a bit, we set off in a mini-bus that reeked of gasoline and emitted a high pitched whirling noise from under the hood.

It was dirt and gravel the whole way. Thirty bone shaking minutes later, we jumped out at in the middle of nowhere and followed a narrow foot path into a wide depression. Gelila hurled himself down the rocks, never missing a step. I followed twenty paces behind, working the decline on all fours like a chimp.

About half way down to the valley floor, Gelila stopped. "Look there," he pointed, "the walls to the temple."

Scanning the foreground, I looked for a collection of upturned blocks and an opening to a subterranean chamber, but there was nothing. It was only after moving closer that a stone wall became apparent. The workings were similar to the Queen of Sheba site, though considerable smaller in scale; field rocks stacked and tiered off with flat gray stone.

"You got to be kidding," I murmured under my breath, and then envisioned those three ten dollar bills swirling around in a wash basin before being sucked down the drain.

"Come, come." Gelila commanded. "The big blocks are on the other side."

Just over the hill was a collection of upturned and dislodged stones similar to the masonry of the Temple of the False Door. There were two more finished stones set in the soil directly below the first group. Now we're talking, I thought to myself.

By now, a small boy and girl had materialized. Gelila said they lived at a nearby farm. So, I dispatched the boy to recover a pick axe and a broom. Upon return, the boy broke away the top layer of dirt and Gelila followed through, sweeping aside the loose soil to expose three tightly fitted stone blocks.

Stooping down, Gelila ran his finger along the thin joint between the blocks, "I believe this to be a tomb."

"Is it a vault that goes back up under the hillside," I asked. "Or just one body underneath these rocks?"

"That, I am not sure," he responded. "But it's a tomb and the other is a temple built later."

"Ask that kid if he thinks there's any gold stashed up under here," I said, as my imagination began to run.

"No! No, don't say that!" Gelila's head snapped around and his eyes filled with angst. "If they think there's gold, they will dig it up tomorrow."

"Um, hmmm," I acknowledged, half chuckling.

Maybe I jumped the gun a little, but you couldn't help wondering what pulling up the rocks might reveal. A body wrapped in brittle cloth, layered with trinkets and other precious items? Or were these the cover stones to a vault that held an even heavier booty?

"How did you find out about this place?" I asked Gelila, feeling a bit better about my expenditure.

"Last year, a Christian man from a Caribbean island came," he began. "He has a list of kings and knows many sites in this valley."

"Are there any more blocks like this?"

Gelila turned to the small boy and spoke in Tigray, the language of northern Ethiopia. The conversation went back and forth a couple of times and then Gelila translated what he'd learned.

"He's saying there is another block they found in the river. It is just at their home. Can we go?"

Traversing further down the hill side brought us to a walled compound with several huts inside. The boy rushed in the largest. After a few moments, he hauled out a block of refined stone.

"Look," Gelila pointed at a peculiar notch in its side. "This has been worked to fit with another stone. It must be part of a large temple."

When the kid erupted in the local tongue again Gelila announced, "They have discovered a small coin too."

"Then get it!" I shouted.

The boy darted back into the hut and then returned with a small match box. Sliding it open, he dumped the contents into the palm of his hand.

"That is an old silver coin!" Gelila announced. Snatching it from the boy's palm, he examined both sides of it closely. The front side showed a profile of a man wearing a crown. There was a second profile on the back, but this time wearing a cloth cap.

"Look, this is written with the old style Geez characters," Gelila said, and then pointed to a small object on the lower portion of the coin. "This king is holding a thin cross. It is the stick cross of St. Mateo. The oldest coins will have the Sabaen half-moon on the back. The newer coins will have the cross on one side and the king on the other side. Eric, I believe this to be one of the first Christian coins!"

After flipping the coin a few more times, Gelila hinted it was time to move. We'd been onsite for just over an hour, but before returning to the road, we stopped at the original site one more time.

"The boy said they have been digging here," Gelila indicated, and then stooped down and began scavenging through the loose rocks on the surface.

"Yes, here is the pottery," he said and then assembled a collection of colored pieces. One had a small, but sturdy handle and another showed linear decorations tracing its circumference.

"The red is old, brown is in the middle and black is the most recent," he stated, and then held up a sample of exceptionally refined ceramics. "And this, the thin one, is the oldest of all."

Pottery wasn't the only discovery of the afternoon. A few steps away Gelila began picking vigorously at the reddish brown soil and retrieved several sizable white splinters.

"This is the human bone," he said, while holding the specimen up so I could see the spongy pattern of the hardened marrow.

"So, what do you think?" I asked, looking for his take on the place. Gelila reiterated his theory on the tomb and temple, but then speculated in a larger context, the area may have been used as a venue for the coronation of Axum's earliest kings.

"We will know much more when the Caribbean man returns," he added. "Now let us go. I have one more place to show you."

By the time we got back to the road, a slight chill was in the air. Luckily, a van arrived right away. After a short distance, Gelila and I jumped out and hiked across an open field peppered with fist sized rocks. The scene was like the fallout from a massive volcanic blast. After a couple of stone walls there was a heavily traveled trail that ascended a steep hill. A small village was at the top, but our attention was immediately drawn to a massive stone pillar listing to one side. Further along, there was a second pillar that had toppled over and lay flat on the ground.

While I surveyed the stones, an elderly man approached Gelila and spoke loudly while gesturing wildly with his hands.

"What's the guy saying?" I asked, fearing the old timer was trying to shake us out of some dough.

"I'm just explaining why we are here," Gelila said. "Everything is okay, Eric. We can pass now."

Along the summit of the hill there were more stone columns staggered out in a semi circle around a depression. A couple of stones were still intact, but most were fractured or toppled. One had been incorporated into a home. The pit had been slowly filling in, like a sinkhole. The large blocks bore resemblance to the site next to Yeha Temple and the layout was reminiscent of the famous megalithic site in the northern hemisphere.

"So what's the story behind little Stonehenge?" I asked.

"We call this Hawulte," Gelila said, while looking over the remains. "The first two stones we passed were part of the gate. This, I believe to be the remains of another temple."

"It seems like someone was digging here," I commented. "I wonder if they found anything."

Gelila conversed with the old man again before answering the question.

"He says this spot was excavated in the 1950's. The archaeologists discovered a gold lion and a gold mask of a man's face."

"Was it Francis Anfray?" I asked. The French archaeologist had completed many excavations in both Eritrea and Ethiopia.

"You know, Eric," Gelila began. "When these people see white, they always think Italian. So, sometimes it is difficult to verify."

By now, the sun was dipping on the horizon. So, we made our way back to the road and flagged down a ride back into Axum.

It should be mentioned there are more ruins across the border in Eritrea too. Metera and Qohaito are both home to stone cities dating back to Axumite times. There is also another stelae field in Keskese; the monoliths at this site are thought to predate Axum. However, I was not going to see them. Next stop was further south to visit a collection of monolithic churches.

V

Lalibela

The flight to Lalibela took thirty minutes. From the air, Ethiopia's rugged terrain became fully apparent. A slow push from deep within the earth formed flat topped mountains with cliffs on all sides. In other spots jagged ridgelines gave way to deep ravines. Soon it becomes apparent why bus travel can take days in the north. Deep bowls lay devoid of habitation causing you to wonder what might lay hidden or buried off the track somewhere. In other places, the landscape is terraced so heavily the ground resembled an isometric map.

After landing, a small tractor retrieved the luggage from the plane and dropped it off at the terminal. Snatching my bag mid stride, I headed into the lobby. Hotel representatives clustered around a group of tables. Immediately, I recognized a budget joint from my travel guide. After a bit of chatting the rep agreed to 200 Birr a night (within budget).

"What about taxi fare into town?" I asked, as airport guys are notorious for steam rolling new arrivals.

"That one is 70 Birr," he replied.

Brilliant, considering the guy next to me on the flight said it would be between 100-150 Birr.

Following a beat up track, the airport taxi rolled across a dry and tired landscape. Dusty people wrapped themselves in tattered clothes and dragged along behind goats, cattle and donkeys. It was almost like a Sunday drive until the track narrowed and we started edging our way up the side of a mountain.

Lalibela lay 2500 meters above sea level in the Lasta district of Wollo province. Originally, known as "Roho" the Ge'ez word for pure and clean, the town was renamed Lalibela in the 19th century after a famous king from the Zabwe Dynasty. With exception to several excursions by the Portuguese, the site was rarely visited and remained unknown to the outside world for some time. Reaching the town was a daunting task, for centuries the only way up the hill was by foot or mule. In the 1990's an all weather road was laid down.

The town's main draw is eleven stone churches that have been carved from the living stone (solid rock). They are divided into three groups; the Eastern Group, the Northern Group and a lone sentinel holding down the fort on the southern flank. No one is absolutely sure who cleared away the stone and shaped the churches. The tourist brochure states these structures are the work of Ethiopian craftsmen. It's a valid point, as there are dozens of rock cut churches scattered across the northern reaches of the country that exhibit the same architectural styles found in Lalibela. Local lore suggests the churches are the work of Ethiopians under the direction of King Lalibela, but with a little outside assistance; it is said that angels worked though the night while the labor force slept. Portuguese adventurers were told that it took white men from Egypt 24 years to carve away the rock, but by far, the coolest theory comes by the way of Graham Hancock. While researching his book "The Sign and the Seal" Hancock came to the conclusion that the churches were constructed by Templar Knights.

The rock cut churches consist of three styles of architecture. The most impressive are the free standing monolithic forms. Here, the church stands isolated in a courtyard mounted on a multi-tiered plinth connected only at the base to what's called the living rock. The second style is semi-monolithic, where the structure is solidly connected to the rock by the base, but also linked to the stone mass on the sides or the roof. Lastly, there are several instances where the church has been excavated from the side of a rock wall or cliff and the exterior is marked by an ornate facade. In technical terminology, these excavations are known as a "hyperum".

Scholars speculate the construction of the church complex was an attempt at creating a second Holy Land so Ethiopian Christians could visit Jerusalem unmolested by Muslim brigands.

However, there is some argument that prior to being a church many of these buildings served a different purpose. This will be discussed as we conduct the tour.

There is a lot of ground to cover in Lalibela. So, it's easy to miss some of the finer details. As a companion to visiting the site check out David W. Phillipson's "Ancient Churches of Ethiopia". A student of Ethiopian History, Phillipson uses this book to take an in depth journey into the rock cut churches of northern Ethiopia. Aside from a wealth of information, his book is packed full of detailed pictures and schematics that show the interior layouts of the churches. Several chapters are specifically dedicated to Lalibela.

Cresting the summit, we rounded through Lalibela, dropping off the other passengers and then arriving at my hotel last. To prevent harm, injury or self-loathing to the simple, feeble minded, or socially challenged, the hotel will be known as the Blue "H" from here on out.

The Blue H had a rustic quality and an obscured view of the valley. The satin purple and lime green blankets were a bit dated, but the bed had clean white linen. The place was contained, but the water pressure was questionable and a big sheet of extra strength plastic was spread across the floor. Half witted, but seemingly with good intent, the gardener bellowed, "Ah-merica!" every time we crossed paths.

For better or for worse, the most notable trait of the place was the sound system. It went off every evening around 8 pm and pounded until the early morning. The music was so loud it seemed like the speakers were wired directly to the front door.

The first night, I just lay in my bed and wondered what irresponsible youth would turn the music up so loud and infringe on the guests. The second night I let it run a bit. Now, I don't mind the gentle grind of background music, but by 10 pm, enough was enough. So, I trekked next door to see what was going on.

Three ladies were seated outside; downtrodden hookers who'd been decommissioned prematurely, reminiscing on the glory days of big boom systems, flashing lights, flashier outfits and the financial rewards of the cash-for-love scene. An evening of chewing khat had produced a glossy sheen across wide opened eyes. They looked on vacantly while I explained the volume was interfering with my sleep.

"Could you turn it down a bit," I asked a second time.

The most alert of the trio nodded slowly and then drifted indoors. After the music went down, she re-emerged with that same blank look on her face. Satisfied with the resolve, I headed back to the sack, but no less than twenty minutes later, the music started back up. As the beat kept pounding I vowed to find a better place. Yeah, it was their spot and probably a nightly routine, but if a guest says it's causing sleep deprivation, then common sense dictates to keep it down until they move on.

The next morning, I went up to a joint called Lalibela Hotel and explained the issue.

"No problem," the manager laughed. "We make for you 250."

"Bet!" So, I marched back down to the Blue H, rounded up my gear and sent word to the manager I was checking out.

Beaten down from the previous night's action, she emerged from a back room in a stale mode. After accepting payment, she shuffled aimlessly through a stack of papers and pounded blindly on a calculator.

"You must pay more," she snarled.

"Taxi man said 200 a night," I protested. "Call the guy and let's sort it out."

"Just wait! Just wait!" She panicked.

What for, I wondered and then handed her the balance for two nights, but she tried to string me out for more dough. Sure, I could have left without the receipt, but who knows; maybe she was in with crooked cops just waiting to profit on a foreigner.

"Get that guy on the phone!" I yelled, tired from the delay.

A few moments later he was there, "No worries, my friend. Pay 400 Birr and you'll get receipt."

"It's done!" I confirmed, and then passed the phone back to the friendliest receptionist in all of Northern Ethiopia.

After spouting a profanity laced tirade into her mobile, she scribbled out a receipt and then tossed it at me. Now that the formalities are out of the way, it was time get to the ruins!

VI

Cut Rock

Follow the cobblestone road up the hill to get to the site's main entrance. You will pass by the churches, but don't get any funny ideas. There is a guard at each one and they'll demand to see your ticket upon entry. Along the way, idle youth and street urchins will badger their way into your itinerary. The most common phrases of engagement are "From where do you come?", "Do you know Premier League?", "Can I help you?" and "Sir, can I shine your shoes?"

Any attempt at pushing things off a day or two is followed by, "Promise? Sir, do you promise?"

There are no promises!

When not terrorizing tourists and travelers these rascals can be found crowding ping pong and pool tables, or, the old rod and roll Foosball games. Remember those?

It cost fifty bucks to see the rock churches. This may seem steep, but the pass is valid for four days, giving you ample time to get your money's worth. Now, I have to warn you, upon first sight you may be disappointed. About half of the churches are shielded by large metallic canopies with long legs anchored in the bottom of the courtyards. These monstrosities were built for conservation reasons, but they are a distraction of the highest order. As stated earlier, the reason we're here is to see the wear and tear of Mother Nature against the work of man, that's what makes them ruins.

After crossing into the grounds a skinny bloke stepped forward and asked if I needed help with a tour.

"Will you take ten bucks?" I replied.

"No, I cannot," he said, and then shook his head mildly.

"Ok, then twenty."

"That is too small," he sighed. "I must have thirty-five dollars for the guide fee."

Whew, that was out of my league. So, I had to pull the chute on him. "In that case, I'm just going to have to fly solo."

It was a wise choice, because the fun of Lalibela would come in exploring all the tunnels and passages that interconnect the churches. Having a wing man would have just slowed me down.

The first church on the circuit was Bet Madhane Alem. To fully appreciate this specimen, you have to trudge carefully along the ledge and look down into the pit. If someone asked for a one word description of this church, it would have to be "beast". It's an immense 33.7 X 23.7 X 11.5 meters. Thirty-four columns are spaced out along the four sides of the structure. Most were replaced in 1954, but a few of the originals still stand along the backside. An arcade of arches runs above the columns on all four sides too. Down in the courtyard, Bet Alem exudes the appearance of a lost temple on a remote island in the Aegean Sea. Its fortified appearance will have you wondering if there is hoard of gold vaulted away down below.

Chunks of the old workings are scattered around the narrow court yard separating the church from the rock. A cross-hatch pattern scarred the rock walls enclosing the place. It's easy to imagine a legion of sweaty backs, dusty faces, and calloused hands chipping away layer-after-layer of over burden with implements of crude iron.

Visitation at the church has been so intense the rock floor at the main entrance has been polished to a smooth finish. You have to remove your shoes to get inside. The interior is dimly lit and the air is cool and motionless. Significant portions have been curtained off, but you can see a small altar in the front with large religious paintings positioned on either side of it.

Next, hop through the cut in the wall directly across from the main entrance. The short tunnel leads to a large courtyard with three other churches, Bete Mariam, Bete Meskel and Bete Danigal.

Though considerably smaller than its neighbor, Bete Mariam is a stout monolithic church distinguished by its architectural features. Three stone porches extend from the north, south and west walls. The window styles vary; several are cut in the style of a swastika, but possibly the most thought provoking feature is an engraving over the south porch. It's a bit worn down these days, but with a little focus you will see two charging horsemen. The piece is believed to be an early rendition of St. George slaying the dragon. Bete Mariam's interior is characterized by murals of biblical scenes, animals, and a painting of a double-headed eagle.

Portions of the courtyard's north wall have been hollowed-out to form the cave like Bete Meskel. Protruding from the southern wall is Bet Danigal, another grotto like excavation. Although it is simple in design with little decoration, locals claim the church is in dedication to fifty nuns killed by a Roman Emperor. Another story claims it serves as a memorial to the thirty-six female followers of Jesus Christ.

Exit the compound through the south wall and then hang a right, the narrow passage leads to the last zone in the Northern Complex. It is comprised of two churches, Bete Debre Sinai, Bete Golgotha and a spot called Adam's Grave. Of the two, Bete Golgotha is the more distinguished. It is home to a collection of bas relief figures. There are tombs for Jesus Christ and King Lalibela. Tucked away inside the church, the Trinity chapel holds three monolithic alters decorated with figures of a man, lion, eagle and a bull.

This area is also full of deep trenches and narrow pathways that span overhead. After landing on high ground, you'll be approached by one of the holy men that congregate in the area. He'll guide you into a chamber where you can take pictures of him in ceremonial dress while holding a large gold cross.

Afterwards, top up the donations bowl with a dash; you don't want the lads to go thirsty, do you?

Reaching the Eastern Group of churches is a bit of a hike. You have to trek across a massive rock embedded in the hillside, up some stairs and then over a stout bridge that spans a chasm filled with brackish water. Along the way, the flies burrow into your nose and buzz around your mouth kamikaze style. With all the donkey dung piled up around the place, who knows what these little pests were slogging through before attacking.

On the other side of the bridge there are two routes of travel. A narrow path called the Stairway to Heaven continues up the hill. At the top there is a collection of stone blocks arranged in a defensive position. The main route dips down into a narrow grotto that faces the next church, Bete Gabreal.

Some have speculated that this church was originally carved out as a regal residence or a treasury. Considering there's a second bridge to cross before reaching the entrance, they might be right (check out the crucifixes carved in rock before heading over). Bete Gabreal's façade consists of a series of buttresses and recesses that run vertically from the bottom of a seventeen meter deep court. At roughly the ten meter mark, there are two platforms that span the width of the façade. Due to the internal structural disposition, Bete Gabreal is now connected with another church, Bete Rafael.

After a short visit, walk further on into the cave. It turns into a tunnel that twists higher, to the right, and then into another grotto. Here you'll push open a massive wooden door reinforced with iron studs. Just beyond, a flight of steps leads up and out into the open, but not for long. Follow the dusty trail to a narrow pit. Here you'll plunge down a stair case hacked out of the rock. At the bottom, take a right and pilot your way through a V-cut passage until you cross a wood bridge.

After admiring a round chamber with a series of rectangular windows, slip into the hole in the wall; it's called the Tunnel to Hell. The light fades out after a few steps. Soon you're swallowed up by the darkness. Don't go for a flash light; allow yourself a few minutes to be completely absorbed by the void. You should be disorientated, unable to determine up, down, backward or forward. Could you imagine being a trapped miner waiting for the rescue team after a cave in? Or, say you got lost spelunking and your batteries died out. It would be impossible to fully comprehend the horror and agony of being lost or pinned beneath a rock deep within the Earth and wondering when or if someone was coming to rescue you. Now, let's move forward to the next objective.

While pressing ahead, remember to keep your hands high because there is an outcrop up on the right. If you're not looking for it, that rock will reach out and find you. Once past it, the tunnel will trend downward for a bit. It's almost like you're lost in the bowels of the Earth, but just keep shuffling forward. An obstacle on the left will bust your knee cap, but don't mind it. In a few moments, a faint patch of light will illuminate the rock ahead. Now that you've found the end, the only way out is by pulling yourself up a set of steep and uneven steps to emerge upon Bete Merkerios.

Bete Merkerios is a subterranean chamber of which its reputation stands on twenty columns in various stages of existence (several have collapsed). Outside is a large courtyard that yielded shackles during some excavations in the 1960's. Originally, this church is thought to have served a municipal function.

After a brief survey, follow the next tunnel further into the site's historicity. The dip leads to a set of uneasy steps, but once on the bottom you'll be in awe of the geometric complexity of Lalibela's third monolithic church.

Wherein the other churches display certain features of Aksumite architecture, Beta Ammanuel is a prime specimen. Stone ribbing in the form of protruding and receding lateral bands run parallel around the churches four sides. There are three rows of windows, all in the Aksumite style, most notable the stele formed windows of the middle row. Monkey heads abound at every opportunity.

It's like there's a riddle worked into the design of this massive cube. Anyone with the proper understanding of repetition, angles and degrees may unlock esoteric knowledge from the past. It is also said that there is a trap door in the church that opens to a tunnel back to Bete Merkerios. When you're finished admiring the magnitude of the place, slide out the porthole in the back, glide down the narrow trench and then pass through a sliver tunnel.

On the back side of the northern complex lay Bete Abba Libanos. Amongst the smaller churches, it is free-standing on all four sides yet still connected to the living rock at the roof. There is almost ten meters of stone overhead. The churches façade is an arrangement of windows and vertical bands in the Aksumite style, very similar to Bete Ammanuel. In fact, the church could be the precursor to much larger calculations. Some say Abba Libanos was built as a memorial to King Lalibela by his wife. There is also a rumor that the church's altar is illuminated at all times by a mysterious source of light.

Having nearly completed the circuit, I scaled a nearby hill to get the lay of the land. Just as I was ready to absorb the ambience of a striking vista (the rugged lines of distant hills drifted away and dissipated into the blue haze of a fading horizon) my concentration was brutally interrupted.

"Hallo! Hallo!" A man with a tight face and slight build called out while approaching my position. He wore a gray pull over, urban camouflage trousers and soiled combat boots.

"Yeah?" I answered sternly.

"From which place do you come?"

"States," I replied, still deliberating on what tact to take with this intrusion. "The good ole USA."

"America! I know the place," he acknowledged seriously. "What profession do you make?"

Slowly, I explained that I'd spent the last two years providing remote technical support for the employees of a big international company.

"I was the night guy," I smiled back, half warming to the conversation. "What's your job?"

"Me, I was in Ethiopian Army from 1990. Now, I am with National Police."

"I bet you like that AK-47, don't you?"

"No, we used AKM and RPG!" he declared, and raised his arms like he was shouldering a rocket launcher.

"I fought in the Eritrean War. Many friends died there," he grimaced. "They wont be back."

"That's awful," I replied, but now fully tuned in to the discussion. His description of fire arms had piqued my interest. On the ride in from the airport, I'd spotted a man with an SKS rifle and was curious about its status amongst the civilian population.

"It ok," he confirmed. "That one only carries ten bullets, good for hunting only. Do you hunt?"

"No," I answered. "But I dust off my .22 carbine lever action with the large loop from time-to-time and hit the plinking range with my buddies."

"How can you not hunt?" he asked, as his face sagged in disbelief. "I am a very good hunter. I was even sharp shooter in the army."

"You are champion!" I shouted, and then indicated I had to be going and made my way to the final church.

"Learn to hunt!" He replied, and then waved his finger at me.

Standing solo on Lalibela's southern flank, Bete Giogyios takes the form of a cross from top to bottom. The right proximity of the courtyard walls in relation to the church's slender design makes you feel like you're standing next to a skyscraper in a pit. The church has twelve sides and two rows of windows. The bottom row has nine blind windows and the top row has twelve windows and the roof sloops slightly with the grade of the rock. From a nearby perch, you can view the cross design in the roof. It resembles the cross on a Templar Knight's shield; perhaps Graham Hancock was right.

Bete Giogyios is considered to be in the best condition of all the churches. Some have referred to it as Lalibela's best offering.

However, I disagree. After completing the tour, I found Bete Ammanuel to be the most interesting.

Now that my work in the northern front was completed, it was time to move south. The following morning I'd be flying to Ethiopia's capital city, Addis Ababa. From there, it was on to explore a couple of interesting sites away from the beaten track.

VII

Butajira

After landing in Addis I bullied the taxi drivers until I got a reasonable rate to the bus station. There, I grabbed the last seat on a fleabag bus making the run south to Butajira. The ride was uneventful except for a lengthy delay caused by some traffic police looking for beer money and a sickly mama who head butted me every time she nodded off. At the bottom tier of transport, challenges were to be expected. So, the physical contact wasn't so much a bother. It was the gurgle of loose phlegm whenever she coughed that had me on edge.

After three hours of spinning the tires, the bus arrived at Butajira and I made camp at the Bright Hotel. An Ethiopian guide had referred me to the place while in Lalibela. So far, I just racked out and then paid the balance at check-out. This place wanted the cash up front every day, but at 150 Birr a night, this was a score.

With exception to the TV set, the room was functionally correct. The locks on the cabinet worked and it still had both keys. In the bathroom, the sink fixtures were securely in place, the toilet fully intact and in proper working order. Also, the shower pumped out a steady stream of scalding hot water. So, I mugged these guys for a twenty-five minute shower every single day!

There was a bit of a language gap, but the staff was friendly, the service was good and the food tasted great. For instance, the French Toast was deep fried and served vertically in a glass gobbler, but that was nothing compared to the Beef Burger. I needed a forklift to get the damn thing off the plate!

The hotel was in a large three-story building. I took a room on the top deck looking down on the main drag. Buses and trucks barreled through town. The sound of tooting horns, accelerating motor cycles and the din of hundreds of conversations going down all at once reverberated everywhere.

At ground level, the stench of stale urine hung in the air, eclipsed only by the smoke trail of burning rubbish. One-man shops set in tin roof shacks met the daily necessities of life: food, shelter and clothing. New multi-level props were going up and being christened with contemporary names like "Mars Tower". Where there had been few in Axum and none in Lalibela, here women wore long dresses and head scarves of the Islamic caliber, and the men, small caps notched tightly down on their skulls. Darker faces with Bantu features where now prevalent.

Tourism wasn't a strong point in this town, made evident by all the inquisitive stares I got. Most residents had little understanding of English. So, there was a lot of slowly pronounced phrases and sign language. Every so often, some fellow would stand up along the roadside, point at me and shout "you" and then sit back down again. I never figured that one out.

Town life died down about 10 pm every night; crazy people howled through the nocturnal hours. They made themselves known when the sun was up too. The day I arrived, a man paced in the middle of the road flagging down vehicles or ambushing those idling on the shoulder for hand outs. Then there was the bloke who took off his shoes and jumped down into the gutter (it was two and half feet deep), lit a fire and then emptied the contents of his bags. After restocking his kit he bolted down a side street leaving the flames unattended, no one cared. The best was the woman with the size double-Ds who disrobed at high-noon and started jumping up-and-down in place. That got everyone's attention.

VIII

The Tiya Stones

After a day of R-and-R spent toiling around town, I set off to visit a local site called Tiya. As the transport filled up, a thin girl in overalls and a big straw hat worked the mini-buses selling bottles of soda. Since the glass is needed to reclaim the deposit, she emptied the contents into a 500 ml plastic bottle and then passed the drink off to her customer.

Throughout Africa industrial goods of mass production live multiple lives; plastic drink containers are no exception. They're picked out of dust bins, road sides and empty lots time-and-time again. Chances are it was on its third term. Upon finishing the beverage, that jug gets tossed out on the ground and then is scooped up again. If it's lucky, it might even get rinsed out before being redeployed.

Forty-five minutes later, I jumped out at a wide spot in the road and followed the signs back to the site. Immediately, I was set upon by a curator looking for the entrance fee. After receiving payment, he started working me over for a guide fee.

"Not now," I responded. I wasn't up to being sliced for 100 Birr at the start.

The site is boxed in by a square wire fence strung along concrete posts. The only thing missing were the loops of barb wire along the top and guard towers in the corners. Inside the yard, roughly hewn stones with symbols crudely engraved into the front are lined up in a couple of groups. Overhead the sun bore down like a camp commandant making misery for sport.

Unimpressed by the stones, I headed over to the curio stand and checked out the locals. There was a mom with a snot nosed kid and a couple of idlers camped out in the shade. One was a looker too. After a smile and introduction, she agreed to escort me back out to the monoliths.

Eighteen years old and full of energy, she had her sights on studying history in England, but right when the conversation started getting interesting the caretaker came storming across the pitch.

"The ticket is good for one visit only," he sternly announced. "You must pay for another ticket!"

"What?" I shouted back. Was he so worried about losing his shake he wanted to double dip on the entrance fee?

"Look, pal," I started, "you got me all wrong. I was going to circle back around and grab you for the tour. It's just that I bumped into this missus right, and I er...ah, well you know."

"You will pay fifty Birr for guide?" he asked, still stinging from the fear of being undercut.

"Of course, buddy."

"No problem," he smiled. "Shall I call her for you?"

By now the dame had drifted back to the souvenir stand.

"You're already here, brother." I responded. "So, we might as well get started."

"This place was discovered in 1905," the curator began, as we walked to the first group of stones. "At that time it was all forest here. In 1974, the first excavations commenced."

"What kind of stuff did they dig up?" I asked.

"Many things," he replied.

"Like what?"

"Like obsidian, axes, knives, bracelets and rings. They have also found fifty-one bodies in the fetal position and one flat."

The body in the horizontal position indicated he was buried after the main group, probably sometime during the Christian era.

At the main assemblage of monoliths, one stood out from the rest. Laying flat on the ground was a large stone with marks representing jewelry, tattoos and traditional decorations. Anatomically, there were two skinny arms on the sides and a pair of sagging breasts reminiscent of the good old days in National Geographic

Magazine. The fractured remains of a face and headdress were positioned nearby.

"That's African mother proper, yeah?" I said, with a light snicker.

"Yes, yes." The curator chuckled back. "It is true."

"How many monoliths are there?" I asked, interested in knowing the extent of the standing rock in these parts.

"One hundred and fifty in the nearby hills," he responded while pointing to a ridgeline in the distance.

It's said there are thousands of monolithic stones dotting the country side. In fact, there are two other major sites a few hours south of Butijira. Tutu Fella is a cluster of over 80 stelae with a variety of decorations and another site, Tututi, has specimens topping out at 7.5 meters in height.

Moving to the final set, the curator kneeled down and pointed to one with multiple symbols.

"When we look at this one, we see he was very strong," he began, and then counted the markings. "This one has killed nineteen in battle. Very strong!"

It was true. Most stones only had one or two swords. This guy had more than all combined.

As the narrative died down, I paid the curator his money and then headed back to the road. There was one more site to visit in Ethiopia. After that I'd be on a big bird in the sky heading south into Kenya.

IX

Areshetan, the Lake of the Devil

During my stay in Butajira people kept mentioning a place called Areshetan, or, simply, the Lake of the Devil. Word was a local body of water had a penchant for eating people. There was also this thing about disappearing stones, a shaman and a sacred cave; all the makings of a portal for inter-dimensional travel. So, through conversation with the hotel's head waiter, Azezew, and I made a tentative deal to visit the lake. Initially he wanted 400 Birr to guide the excursion. I worked him down to 250, but was still paying through the nose and dissatisfied with the arrangement. By chance, I got to talking to the night clerk, Tadele, a tall slender lad with big curly hair and heavy eye brows.

"I know the place very well." He smiled broadly and agreed to take me there for 100 Birr. That was more like it, so, I quickly reorganized.

A smallish man with a round head, Azezew showed his displeasure openly when informed of the new arrangement. I couldn't blame the guy for being bent out of shape, but I had to assess things from my perspective. Tadele communicated English fairly well and Azezew did not. Also, he intended to bring in another guide who didn't speak English at all. Additionally, tensions started to brew between the two and their disagreement was beginning to spill out in the work place. So, it seemed wise to make some kind of compromise.

"Gents, how about this," I proposed. "The three of us make the trip together; I'll give you each 100 Birr and cover transport costs. Ok?"

Both men nodded in approval and the deal was set.

Later on that afternoon, we boarded a tuk-tuk and then headed out into the countryside. After alighting, we made a tact on a series of low lying hills, but almost from the outset, there was a bit of confusion. Azezew changed paths several times, unsure of which direction to continue on.

"Do you know where you are going?" Tadele bore down on him with clenched eye brows.

"Yes, it is this side," Azezew squirmed, and then pointed up at the hills.

Unconvinced, Tadele rebutted in Ahmaric and soon both men were standing toe-to-toe in disagreement.

While the two of them thrashed things out, an old lady crept along the foot path.

"Areshaten?" I inquired, and tossed both hands up in the air.

"Areshaten!" She answered and then pointed back at the road.

"There, you see," Tadele snapped. "It is that direction."

"OK," Azezew acknowledged sheepishly.

"For now on, follow me only!" Tadele said under clenched teeth as he headed back towards the road.

After flagging down a mini-bus, we advanced to a drop-off point further out. Following a narrow dirt road we passed through a collection of cone roofed huts. Throngs of children poured out of the dwellings and squawked, "Give me money!"

Tadele snarled menacingly at the kids and then turned to me. "They think money is just there."

Excellent observation, I thought, and happy to know a local shared my point of view.

Initially, the landscape had a gentle grade, but as we reached the hill, it took on a sharper incline. The soil was much darker than the northern regions of Ethiopia and the ground was peppered with many rocks; the density increasing as we moved forward.

"Fifty meters," Azezew indicated, bringing himself back into the picture.

"Ten meters," he announced a few steps later, and then continued to countdown the distance until we reached the top of the hill.

The summit gave way to a vista overlooking an elliptical crater filled with murky green water. In geological circles, this type of physical feature is known as a phreatic explosion crater. Two sets of cliffs ringed the lake and a steep path jogged down into the crater; one bad step could send you on a tumble.

As Azezew and I surveyed the lake, Tadele slipped into the background and then returned holding a large stone.

"Now we will see," Tadele announced, and then wound up and tossed the projectile with unrestrained vigor. Anxiously, the three of us waited to see the ripple effect of a rock hitting the water, but there was nothing.

"You see," Tadele shouted with certainty. "The stone has disappeared."

Azezew looked at him in disappointment, and then shook his head. "You are not energetic."

After a few moments of rummaging around he came up with a few tennis ball sized rocks. Tossing one to me, he then looked at Tadele, "Now I will show you."

Azezew made a couple of dry runs and then let loose with a solid throw. Again, we waited for the ripples in vain. Using his second rock he tried again, but no effect.

Now it was my turn. Starting back a bit, I stepped forward and pitched the rock with all my might. Confident that I'd score I could barely contain a smile, but when the ripples failed to appear the other two were absolutely convinced of the rock's disappearance.

"Guys," I began. "There's no way a rock is just going to disappear. It's just not going to happen."

"Then what is it?" Tadele asked, still confused.

"First, the distance to the water is probably a lot further than it looks. Second, have you noticed the head wind?" The entire time, a steady breeze and been blowing across the crater into our faces. "We're simply not getting enough oompf to surpass these two obstacles."

"Oompf?" Azezew echoed in a perplexed way.

"Yes," I said. "Oompf is that little extra something that makes us big winners in life."

They both nodded hesitantly, unsure of the definition, but kind of enjoying the explanation.

Now that one phenomenon had been solved, it was time to get to the bottom of the other. "So, let's hear it, gents. What about these missing people?"

Responding simultaneously, Azezew and Tadele told the story of a newly wedded couple who decided to take a swim after their marriage ceremony.

"Upon entering the water," Tadele stated, "they disappeared below the surface and never came back up."

"To this day," Azezew added. "The remains have not been recovered."

Glancing back down at the brackish waters, it was easy to imagine the lair of some unforgiving beast, that when disturbed, rose to the surface, latched on to the jubilant swimmers and then squeezed the last bubbles of air from their lungs while tugging them down into the depths. Or better yet, perhaps the lake was an entrance to a secret subterranean UFO base where any violators were abducted and used for ghastly experiments.

"Come sir," Azezew tapped my shoulder and indicated the next objective. "We must go quickly."

Normally, I prefer taking my time at such places, but the two of them had to report back to the hotel no later than 5 pm and it was almost four. So, we trudged higher to the top of another hill. His confidence regained, Azezew leading the charge with Tadele on his heels and me, pulling up the rear. My thighs were burning, lungs on the verge of exploding and my feet hanging up on every little pebble, stone or rock.

After cresting a second summit, we descended into a small crater overgrown with forest. The environment was cool and relaxing and the floor of the depression took on a steep decline that led down to a massive fracture in the earth. On the far side of the hole, huge vines draped down into the shadows. Dark and jagged, the pit looked like the secret entrance to Pellucidar, Edgar Rice Burroughs' fictitious world within a hollow earth.

Diligently, we followed a path that hugged the crater wall and found a shallow cave. Inside the grotto, an older man with a five o'clock shadow sat silently on the ground. He wore cheap sunglasses, many layers of clothing and a white cap with gold embroidering.

"This is Silti Aynagie Cave," Tadele whispered, and then squatted down on a rock. "We must remove our shoes."

"What?"

"Yes," Azezew reiterated. "It is true."

Upon entering the cave, there was an eruption of double clasp handshakes, hugging and cheek banging. Tadele took the brunt of it while I lagged behind worrying if fleas would burrow into my socks and feed on my ankles. Finally, it was my turn to greet the old man; I did my best at maintaining a buffer zone.

Keeping a safe distance, I settled in and surveyed the furnishings. Battered tarps hung from the cave walls and woven mats and dingy goat skins were spread out on the ground. The broken remains of cast iron cooking gear were strewn about and a tired set of coffee ceremony utensils awaited resurrection.

Tadele and Azezew began conversing with the man. He had been living in the cave for 27 years, had multiple wives and 8 kids. This might have explained why he was so boisterous. Every time I spoke he mimicked me in a loud and obnoxious way which was starting to put me off. Another annoying mannerism was the way he picked at his feet. Was he doing that before shaking my hand?

"How deep is that pit?" I asked while pointing at the downward slope.

"Over sixty-seven meters," Tadele answered and then said something to the monk.

The old man got to yapping and indicated there were caverns leading into southern Ethiopia and another that tunneled all the way to Yemen (yes, under the Red Sea!).

"We have yet to confirm that," Azezew interjected, "but it is there."

Fascinating stuff, I thought, but ever since taking my shoes off, I was getting the creeps and wanted to get out there. Discreetly pointing at my watch, I indicated to Tadele it was time to roll. He acknowledged by rubbing his finger tips together; we had to slip the old bugger some dough. In Morse-code-like succession,

I flashed five three times with my hand; his eye brows raised up in agreement.

After lacing up our shoes, Tadele slid the monk 15 Birr and Azezew led the way up and out of the crater. Despite some minor complications, the afternoon had turned into a splendid little jaunt.

Kenya: the Party

X

Touch Down

Atieno and I had met a couple of years back through a mutual acquaintance. We'd maintained contact via Facebook; the correspondence growing steadier as my departure time for Africa neared. When she learned I'd be traveling through Kenya, Atieno insisted I visit her in Port Rietz. Before leaving we shared some thought provoking emails. So, I was anxious to see her.

She met me at the airport in a tight fitting black track suit and running shoes. Long thin braids draped from her head all the way down to her waist. Her athletic build was accentuated by firm curves in the right places. Atieno's complexion was so rich she could blend into the shadows (her position compromised only when smiling), and, a fresh application of red gloss coated her well contoured lips. Wow! This was one hot Luo gal (Luos are a Nilotic tribe from western Kenya, near Lake Victoria). After greeting each other with a light hug and a peck on the cheek, we loaded into the taxi she had waiting for us.

Back at Atieno's house, I unpacked my bags and began to settle in. As the morning turned to day and the day turned to night the emails and text messages we'd exchanged played out in the best way; through subtle conversation at first. Then, picking up like a gust of wind rustling through the palm trees. Soon, all apprehensions dissipated and the passions of our expectations were unleashed, culminating with the strength and rhythm of ocean waves rolling across a moon lit beach.

Atieno lived in a one story two bedroom home overlooking a small inlet off of Kilidini Harbor. The accommodations came with her job at a state run college. The kitchen and bathroom were utilitarian and the sitting room fully ventilated. Inside, geckos, stubby little lizards with the ability to walk on walls and upside down, darted out from their hide outs and snatched up unsuspecting insects. Outside, there was a big yard and a dilapidated chicken coop. On the waters below, three small tankers and a mid-sized container ship lay anchored, their disposition reflecting the tidal motions.

Okay, the ceiling sagged a little bit and the place was in need of paint and flooring, but by local standards, I was slumming high-on-the-hog. The view was inspiring, the house was in a shady spot with a steady breeze and Atieno cooked up massive plates of food every night.

Moi International Airport lay inland a bit further back. At set times of the day, the whirling roar of accelerating engines would pick up and a passenger jet would climb above the tree line and then veer away to the south; a scene reminiscent of the Millennium Falcon blasting its way out of Mos Eisley.

Like the entirety of the continent, the place had water issues, but Atieno's were further complicated by the neighbors. Not only did they give away water to non-residents and squatters from the same tribe, they completely ignored the leak on their property.

"Kisiis are so arrogant!" Atieno vented whenever the water stopped running (Kisiis are a Bantu tribe from western Kenya). "These are learned people who refuse to take the proper steps and fix the water. Can you believe?"

The next day, Atieno awoke with a massive smile on her face. In fact, after a cup of Chai, that grin carried us all the way down to the water front for some exploration on the back end of Port Reitz.

After negotiating some rough terrain, we landed at the foot of four huge fuel tanks shielded by a massive concrete bunker.

"Who built Noah's Arks?" I asked.

"These ones here?" Atieno responded. "A very powerful man from Nairobi, he could even know Moi." Moi was His Excellency Daniel arap Moi, Kenya's big man for twenty-five years.

"Are they for the ships or the airport?"

"I'm not sure, but they are not being used because of complications."

After a brief inspection of the metal works, we turned our attention to the water front.

"This is Poor Man's beach," Atieno said, as we strolled along the soggy bottoms of low tide.

Hoards of nickel sized crabs scurried across the wet sand and then disappeared into their water soaked burrows. Occasionally, a larger specimen waved his claws defensively, but broke ranks on our advance. Old shoes, abandoned clothes, broken bottles, shredded plastic by the bushel, and medicinal waste peppered the beach.

"Do you see this one?" Atieno pointed down at a hypodermic needle embedded in the sand. "It is for the drugs. These days, there are so many drugs in Mombasa."

Further along, we met a dozen or so fishermen dodging the sun under a makuti topped shelter (makuti is a high pitched roof made from palm fronds). By ten in the morning, it was already sweltering.

"Look at them," Atieno commented. "They are taking Mnazi and its only morning time." Mnazi is the local brew concocted from coconuts and imbibed by village people in copious amounts.

"Habari zenu," I greeted the men as we passed their camp.

"Wel-come," a handful slurred back.

Further on, a teen age girl emerged from the bushes and picked at the trash. Despite wearing a ragged over sized dress, her belly protruded noticeably.

"And her!" Atieno said. "She is already pregnant. Can you believe, young girls come to this place and shag old men for small coins."

Renegotiating the terrain, we climbed back up the hill for the vantage point on Port Reitz proper; a convoluted maze of metal towers, piping and fixtures, massive lift cranes and the banged up superstructure of big ships. Aside from the clang of heavy metal objects the incessant chug of working machines rumbled across the water. Just beyond, you could make out the tallest buildings in Mombasa. After a brief survey, we passed on through a collection of ramshackle huts called Hodi-Hodi Village and then retired to the house for a siesta.

XI

The Hive

The following day, Atieno and I hopped a Matatu and then headed for town. After working the back streets of Port Reitz, the Matatu muscled its way onto a route that led to Mombasa. Originally planned as a two lane thoroughfare, the road was inundated with almost every conceivable mode of transportation, doubling its capacity. Trucks, cars, buses, motorcycles and mini-vans jockeyed tenaciously to advance through the grid lock. When things didn't move fast enough, free thinking individuals plowed into the throngs of pedestrians that streamed along both sides of the road, at times the competitive nature of Kenyan drivers causing the traffic to temporarily mushroom into six lanes.

Twenty-minutes later, we broke free, but once on the island, got snared up again. The grind continued through a mesh of choked lanes, clogged boulevards and stagnant round-abouts. The traffic crept past dozens of low scale concrete buildings that were stacked up back in the '40s and '50s; every other storefront an electronics depot of some sort. Small shadowy markets were tucked away in the alleys and every surface was silted over with the blackened residue of unchecked emissions.

The exact date of Mombasa's founding has been obscured by time, but some type of settlement has existed for over 1,000 years. The earliest maps show a heavily wooded island speckled with towns and military fortifications. Now, with exception to a golf course and a handful of parks, the island is completely built up, including skyscrapers in the Central Business District. Despite the grind of a modern city, Mombasa has a handful of interesting sites. On the north edge of the island there is an old town and the juggernaut called Ft. Jesus (it was heaved into place by the Portuguese in 1415). Mid-town, there's a double set of metal elephant tusks that span Moi Avenue, built in 1956 to commemorate Princess Margaret's (Queen Elizabeth's sister) visit.

Through the centuries, Mombasa has caught the lash from Portuguese adventurers, Turkish pirates and bloodthirsty cannibals. To this day, conflict continues. In 2002, Muslim fanatics car bombed a hotel and attempted to shoot down an El-Al(Isreali) passenger plane. Al Shabaab terrorists announced their presence in 2012 through a hand grenade assault on a night club.

While stuck at one of the busier intersections, Atieno told me a story about two guys who went drinking at Saba-Saba, a notorious corner to be avoided at all times. After a few rounds these guys started looking for girls. One pulls a girl off the corner and takes her for a shag. After finishing their go, he gives her 100 shillings.

"Do you know what happened next?" Atieno asked.

"What?"

"The girl said wait and I'll bring you back your change."

The exchange rate is about eighty Kenyan Shillings for one US Dollar, get it?

On the street corners, Boda-bodas (motorcycles) and Tuk-tuks congregated in small groups awaiting the next fare. In some parts of town, almost all the side walk space was staked out by small scale merchants who set up stands and peddled anything you wanted; clothes, shoes, books, calendars celebrating the reign of disposed dictators and food. The other stuff you want can be found on the street corners at night or the beach during the afternoon. Pedestrians twist, weave and dodge their way through what little space remains to be navigated. Trash collects in the gutter.

After alighting from the Matatu, Atieno steered us to a chemist that sold anti-Malaria pills (at fraction of the cost back home) and then on to the pirate market where I snagged an extra pair of trousers. In case you're wondering, this is the place where the Somalis unload all the gear they get on the high seas at a five-finger discount. Afterwards, we plied across the broken sidewalks and through denuded parks in search of food, Atieno carefully avoiding the shortcuts, for good reason too.

"There is where I got mugged!" She declared, and then stopped me from turning down an alley.

"Do you know the wooden stick?" she asked, referencing a club. "A man hit me over the head and took everything. I was just bleeding."

After pile driving two massive plates of Chicken Biryani (a spicy rice dish of Indian origin) we found a cozy spot in the shade outside of city hall and began discussing nap time possibilities. Suddenly, Atieno abruptly changed the topic.

"Animals in Mombasa are very strange. Look, here." She instructed, and then pointed at an ungulate of the four legged variety drifting through the park. "Where does a goat walk alone? In my village, they always go together. This one can cross Likoni Ferry early in the morning. In the evening, he'll just cross back, all by himself. Do you know a driver would rather hit a human being than one of these goats?"

"What are you talking about?" I asked, slightly aroused from my food induced stupor.

"I'm saying the goat that walks alone is not real. It is a Genie."

Slightly miffed, I asked what would happen if someone tried to eat a goat that walked alone.

Atieno's eyes widened up and her thick beautiful lips pronounced every word in vivid detail, "Yes, yes! One time, there was this Kikuyu (Kenya's dominate tribe) who rounded up all the lone goats at the market. He was taking them to sell in Nairobi. Do you know, by the time he reached Voi there was a knocking from the back of the lorry." Voi was a three hour drive back up Mombasa Road heading towards Nairobi.

"They turned into people?" I half speculated, but framed my response as a question in order to play it safe.

"Imagine, old women and old men who demanded to be taken home!"

As wild as this claim seems, it is one of many, and these tales often involve Ladies of the Evening.

"Ahh, Eric, Mombasa is full of Genies," Atieno continued with enthusiasm. "Another time, there was man who met a beautiful woman one night at a club. The lady took him back to a house where they really enjoyed themselves. The next morning, the man was found naked. Naked on top of a tree! Kenyan News showed it on the TV. They needed a Fire Brigade ladder to get that man down!"

Naked in a tree is a popular theme, but there's another that is just as fantastic. Back in 1997, during my first visit to Kenya, multiple sources, independent of each other and highly reliable, instructed me to take care when fraternizing with women from the Coast.

"Atieno," I reminisced. "Can you believe I was once told that after removing the clothes from a hot babe I could discover she is a goat from the waist down?"

"Or a snake!" She said, profoundly.

Everyday a big yellow sun burned incessantly through clear blue skies. My travelometer indicated 90 degrees in the shade. No matter how much water I consumed, the sweltering heat leached it from my body. Cripes, I could hardly muster up a piss. When I did, it streamed out like watered down pancake syrup. My quads and biceps ached like mad. After a few liters of water, the unpleasantness settled into my kidneys, but this was only the beginning. By the next day, thousands of tiny red bumps began breaking out across my arms and legs.

The initial reaction is to scratch lightly for a little relief, but I'm telling you, don't do it! After that little jab, your finger nails will be deeply embedded in your thigh or on the inside of your elbow just raking away. It's like an addiction and you'll never find satisfaction. Any relief is incredibly short lived and those little dots will fester up into swollen mounds of raw flesh making you feel like a victim of chemical warfare. Cold showers are the only resolve in this case; you just have to give the inflammation time to clear.

A day later, the rash had rooted across my back, chest and forehead and the tops of my feet. Hell, the damn stuff even broke out on the block and tackle and put me out of commission.

"No worries, babyna," Atieno giggled. "We'll just rest for few days, yah?"

XII

Von Lettow's Forgotten Gold

After a week of cooking, I finally rallied up the strength to do a little investigating. One day I caught a Matatu and headed to South Coast. After battling through the slaughterhouse known as Likoni Ferry (I'll elaborate on this later) I boarded another matatu and made the haul down to Lunga-Lunga, a checkpoint on Kenya's border with Tanzania.

The battered Matatu breezed by clusters of thatched roof buildings and massive agriculture projects while gliding around broad open curves. However, the tranquility of the journey ended abruptly when organizing transport to Vanga village.

At Lunga-Lunga the locals didn't think twice about charging foreigners double (or even triple) the going rate. But through persistent negotiations I made a decent score. Not only would the driver take me down and back for only 300 Kenyan Shillings, he'd wait an hour while I scouted out the village.

"You are very strong," the sun-dried face grimaced as I shook his callused hand; he'd hoped to beat for a bit more.

"Bwana, you left me no choice," I grinned, and then hopped on the back of his Boda-Boda (motorcycle taxi) for the final leg to Vanga village.

Vanga is an obscure fishing village nestled in Kenya's extreme south-eastern corner (check it out on Google Earth). It's so close to the border you'd think a steady wind would have pushed it into Tanzania by now. These days the town is best known for a conflict over fishing rights. Whenever the locals enter the Mwamba Midjira fishing belt they come under the scrutiny of the Tanzanian authorities. Aside from the commotion, there's a bit of fascinating history to the place. One of the mass produced travel guides briefly references a German officer from World War I and gold buried somewhere in the sands.

While the English had Lawrence of Arabia, the Fatherland had Colonel Paul von Lettow-Vorbeck, commander of the East African forces. For four and a half years he waged a guerrilla campaign in one of the least known theaters of World War I, German Tanganyika. Made up of German cadre and African Askaris, his force attacked at will and inflicted heavy losses on five different armies: the English,

Rhodesians, South Africans, Portuguese and Belgians. Just when it seemed hopeless von Lettow always led his troops to victory, securing enough provisions, weapons and ammunition to continue the fight. It wasn't until after the armistice was signed on Nov. 12th, 1919 that he brought his troops in from the bush and surrendered.

Barely five minutes down the track, the grit was already gumming up my eyes and caking up in the corners of my mouth. Determined, the driver followed a narrow trail that weaved around massive pot holes and deep ruts. But every so often he misjudged the track, sending a metallic shudder through the motorcycle and knocking my kidneys a couple of notches lower. After 30 minutes of hard angles and abrupt swerving, the dirt track fed directly into Vanga's main street.

Small shops and lazy bodies lined the dusty avenue. As we flashed by, a couple of individuals shouted a greeting. A hundred meters later the driver gripped the brakes and squealed to an abrupt stop just shy of a concrete seawall.

"You must check in," he said soundly, then pointed towards the veranda of the local police station.

Officer Jefferies stood smartly in his olive drab uniform and another man dressed in civilian clothing shuffled a bit as I explained my visit.

"No problem," the policeman said softly with a watchful eye. "Have a look, but take care."

"Asante." Thank you, I replied, and then began the reconnaissance.

Small groups of Swahili fishermen mended blue and red nets stretched out along the waterfront. Half sunk and faded, a number of wooden boats had collected along the sea wall. Those fit for sailing were moored offshore. Beyond the fleet, a dense patch of mangroves buffered the village from the open waters of the Indian Ocean. Traditional life on the coast is fascinating, but the village focal point was the remains of the colonial era.

Simple and robust, the two story building was like a cube. The paint and finished surface had flaked away to reveal the rudimentary blocks used in its construction. Pleasantly arched doors and windows were placed along the exterior while imposing notches were set evenly along the roof. A tangle of woody vines clung to the seaward side and broad leafy vegetation cloaked two thirds of the back. The same guide book that alluded to lost treasure called this the Customs House.

As I made a closer appraisal, there was the unmistakable crunch of compressed gravel on my left flank. One of the locals had emerged from his rat's nest. His eyes were little more than glossy slits and thin stringers of spittle rolled off his lips. Sweat stained clothes stuck to his body and his tentacle-like dreadlocks were peppered with small bits of detritus.

"Welcome to Vanga Ft. Jesus, brother," he slurred.

"Right," I nodded, and then edged my way into the block-house.

Thoroughly gutted, the dank interior reeked of urine and human excrement. Trees had taken root on what remained of the second floor and stringy vines cascaded down from the gaping wounds where a ceiling had once been. This battered hulk had probably sat derelict since the Winds of Change. Despite its deteriorated condition, there was still an air of authority in the place.

It didn't take much to envision a handful of clerks managing the affairs of Empire.

"This is African toilet, man" Dread smirked, as he plowed through the debris strewn floor with bare feet.

Glancing Dread over a second time, I decided to back out into the open. Although sedated, Rasta was unpredictable. He might be a laid back guide. He might pull out a shank or toss a wild haymaker in hopes of commandeering my bag of sensitive items.

Keeping a respectable distance, he shadowed my retreat.

Despite his condition, Dread might have grown up in Vanga and be familiar with the local legends and lore.

"So, where's all the loot, pal?" I pressed.

"What do you say?"

"The General's hidden treasure?"

"Treasure?" His eye lids peeled open, signaling a momentary break from the drug induced lethargy.

"Lost gold, buddy!"

Bewildered, Dread shook his head from side-to-side, "Lost gold?"

This guy was a dud. With the sun dipping low and the sea breeze growing stronger, it was time to decamp, but I had to make another try before heading back to the main road. In a last ditch effort, I decided to hit up the police.

Jefferies watched carefully while his associate went into an explosive pantomime and then spoke.

"You whites carry all this knowledge," he smiled broadly. "We don't hear of such things until you people arrive."

Jefferies confirmed his testimony. "It's true. These things are not known to us."

The window for exploration had closed. So, there was no way to confirm if lost treasure was buried in Vanga. Getting to the bottom of the story could take months if not years. There are the hours of book work and the bureaucratic nightmare of getting permits. You'd need some kind of assistance from the villages, too, but that could be a crap shoot. They might help, obstruct or lead you on some wild goose chase, bleeding you for every dollar they can. Von Lettow's Gold might be the stuff of arm-chair adventure, but there's nothing wrong with a little dreaming. Imagine digging up a water logged crate, busting it open and then watching a stream of shiny Imperial Deutsch Marks pile up in the sand.

XIII

Fontanella and the Tuk-Tuk Getaway

After two weeks of lounging, I had to meet an old friend at one of Mombasa's finer establishments. Via mobile phone, we agreed the BRP (beer rally point) would be at the corner of Moi Avenue and Digo Road. After arriving into town, I jumped out of a matatu at landing zone GPO (the General Post Office) and then found my way through the crowd.

Out on the street, the sign read Fontanella Steak House and Beer Garden. Inside, the guts were an open aired courtyard with two bars and a slew of plastic tables and chairs and potted plants. It's said this place was a hopping joint back in the '70s and '80s, but the faded animal masks mounted on the wall and the cracked disco ball dangling from the ceiling were all that was left of livelier times. These days the place was in a state of disarray. It reeked of urine and the hired help drag-assed around.

Cases full of refrigerated beer were staggered around the bars and crates of empties waited to be picked up and returned to the brewery. A sparse crowd of locals had gathered and an old Mzungu had lassoed up a leggy Kenyan lady dressed in skinny jeans and red high tops.

With exception to the sound of passing traffic the place was docile, until the harsh popping noise of something wet landing in a pot of boiling grease. It went off with a fury, sending a massive white cloud of smoke to drift away from the kitchen. Right when I caught the smell of burning meat a deep vocalization rolled across the courtyard, "Brothaaaaaaaaaaaaaaaaaaaaaaaaaaaaaa!"

Without second guessing its origin, I stood up and replied, "BRUTHAAAAAAAAAAAAAAAAAAAAAAAAAAAAAAAAAAAA AAAA!!"

He had arrived, Dr. Kubwa Mapenduzi, imbiber of copious amounts of fire water, purveyor of fun times everywhere and ardent academic on nocturnal wanderings.

I had two Tuskers (Kenya's top beer) waiting on the table. So, we went right to work, at times the stories flowing faster than the brew. First, reminiscing on taking the overnight bus to an obscure Tanzanian border post with plans on reaching Mt. Kilimanjaro, but our endeavor thwarted by a testy immigrations official.

"Eh, I cant believe how you dressed that guy down. You know, the whole place was wide-eyed and just wondering, who is this mzungu?" Mapinduzi recalled, before mimicking my words. "I've come to see the majestic splendor of Mt. Kilimanjaro....Eric Meee-chelllll...."

In 1997, on my first go in Africa, I had the propensity to address challenging situations by coming off the high rope. "Yeah, but he got me back. Do you remember what he said?"

"Yes," Mapinduzi replied between swigs and then started pointing his finger down at the ground. "If you want to see Mt. Kilimanjaro, just stand there and look!"

By the second beer, we began digging into the stories from Ohio University, our alma matter. "Who was that lady you brought out to Athens?" Mapinduzi started.

"The Kamba girl?"

"Yes, the one with the car."

A nameless face flashed through my mind, but identity didn't matter. You see, we had driven out to see Herr Doktor and his wife, even doing a bit of joy riding, the ladies in the front and us gents in the back with open flask. When I signaled a turn on short order, the girl just jerked the wheel to the right without braking. So, we took on a ninety-degree turn at about forty miles per hour. The tires squealing angrily as the car slid out of control and came to rest on the opposite side of the road.

"Man, that was close," Mapinduzi said, and then surveyed his rapidly diminishing beer. "So, Eric, what brings you to Kenya this time?"

"I'm on a quest, brother. I'm visiting archaeology from Ethiopia all the way to South Africa."

"When did you arrive?"

"Two weeks ago."

"And you havnt even come to Voi," Mapinduzi commented with a bit of disappointment.

"I'm going to Voi!"

"When?"

"Tomorrow, with you," I stated. "And we're gonna hit the cave of skulls, ok?'

"Yes, yes," Mapinduzi said through a light chuckle. "But where will we stay the night."

"I've already organized accommodations."

"In town?"

"You'll see."

After forty minutes, we were each three tubs deep. Wrestling with the invalids for a refill was no longer an option. So, we split. Mapinduzi squaring up the check and then we hustled out in a flash because the waiter forgot to add the last round to the bill. Around the corner we took a tuk-tuk to Nakumatt-Likoni, a massive grocery store where I bought a six-pack of Corona for old time's sake (fifteen bucks, damn!). On the run back up to Port Reitz, Mapinduzi and I cracked open a bottle each and the festivities proceeded with the clank of ice cold glass colliding together.

"How many Bobcat alumni fly down and tear it up like this?" I shouted over the grind of bumper-to-bumper traffic.

"None! Everyone has gone silent, but you."

We were having so much fun, the tuk-tuk driver asked if he could stop and drink a beer with us.

"Baadaye bwana, lakini baadaye!"

By the time we got to Port Reitz the Coronas were finished. So, after another round at a hole in the wall we headed to Atieno's house. As we neared the door, I turned to my brother and said, "Get ready."

Atieno sprang out of the kitchen right as we entered.

"Hi Maaaaaaaaaaaaaaps," she purred, in a feline way.

"Sasa! It's been a long time," Mapinduzi replied and then spun around and looked at me in shock and disbelief.

I haven't mentioned it yet, but a couple years back we all met up one night on the coast. At the time, I was being escorted by a girl I'd met in Nairobi and Atieno was flying solo, Maps was there for the adventure, and we had a designated driver. All active participants were drinking heavily and things got interesting, but you'll hear about that later.

The food was already done, so, we dove right in. Atieno had made fried chicken, a pot of spicy beef stew and a huge bowl of coconut rice. It was the best spread she'd cooked up yet and the three of us devoured it all on the back patio, even scraping the pot clean! For dessert, Atieno had picked up six more Tuskers.

While she cleaned things up, Maps and I grabbed a bottle. Surreptitiously, he signaled me out back so we could hold a gentlemen's conference in a proper field setting. Resting a hand on the fence, he took a big swig of Tusker and then started talking in a subdued and observant manner.

"I'm in shock," he said, and then his eyes brows arched high up and he made a silly grin. "I'm just wondering if this is real, man. Is that really…"

"It's her."

"The same one who chugged five Smironov Ice and kicked off her shoes?"

"It's her."

"Brother, this is too good to be true. You're on the hill, eating big every night, and you've got that hot babe. What is really happening here? I mean, she's walking around calling you sweets. Ehhhhh! This can't be real."

"It's real," I smiled broadly.

Maps choked on some back wash before letting go with a muffled, but solid laugh. "Her lower lip is curving way out and she's always blowing you kisses. Enjoy it brother, but don't forget, this is Kenya," he advised. "What's the plan if funny things start happening?"

Chuckling mildly, I smiled even bigger. "This is Africa, brother. The sun comes up, the sun goes down."

Maps grinned and then took another swig. "That's good, because I'm just wondering how this will play out."

That said, we gravitated back to the house, finished the beers and enjoyed stories with Atieno amidst a Franco jam session that lasted into the wee hours of the night. In fact, the music was so good and so loud the District Commissioner (an administrative position originating from the British Colonial Service) stopped by the next day and asked why he hadn't been invited. Next time, brother!

XIV

Confessions of a Small Time Trader

Just after dawn the following morning Maps and I cruised back into town for a couple of errands and then headed out to Voi.

The trip from Mombasa to Voi takes about three hours. So, now is a good time to tell you about Matatus, Kenya's most common form of transportation. First off they are everywhere and back in the good ole days, they got stuffed to the point of suffocation; body upon body stacked inside and even hanging out the slide door. The bench seats were designed for three people, but in

Kenya, that just means they're supposed to hold four. Onboard, stereos blast high pitched music and the musty aroma of soiled armpits jabs away at your nose.

Under the influence of khat, an agricultural product chewed for its spiritual enlightenment, the drivers operate in complete disregard for common sense, let alone driving laws. As a result, high speed collisions are common and brutal. Upon impact, Matatus can get sheared open like sardine tins; the passengers spilling out on the road like little fishes. Though on the bright side, no matter where you are there's always a ride in Kenya.

At one point, the authorities tried to clean things up. Touts and drivers were issued uniforms and identity cards. Seating regulations and passenger counts were enforced, but only temporarily. In Kenya, money trumps all.

Being that these mini-vans are subject to multiple police shake-downs. The touts(they organize the passengers, cargo and take the money) and drivers are always on the lookout to cover their losses and increase profits. So, they don't think twice about gouging anyone. If you're Mzungu, take care!

A densely packed gas station served as the launch point (known as Voi stage locally). Across the street big air conditioned buses departed for Nairobi. So, this was a major transit point. If you're caught waiting through a joint like this, be prepared for the endless stream of hawkers.

"Mzungu, can you promote me?" Is a common pitch, and you might hear it 15-20 times as they try to unload every and anything on you; soda baridi, maji baridi, woman's handbags, children's undergarments, men's handkerchiefs, bags of apples, oranges and freshly cut sugar cane, little sacks of peanuts and cashews, belts, pirate DVDs, boxes of biscuits, sunglasses and fake leather wallets, just to name a few.

Brash and pesky, these bastards have no boundaries and will thrust an item in your face at will. Battling with them only attracts more. So, instead of smacking their hand away, the best response is "asante" (Swahili word for thank-you) and then looking the other way.

Luckily, a matatu was in the ready-rock position with two empty seats, but they were in the very back.

"Forget it, man," I indicated. Stuck in the back was the worst place to be during a crack-up. Each time I'd been caught in the last seat I had visions of fiery explosions. "I'm not getting in there."

"Mzungu, its okay," the tout said. "Come, sit here."

Yanking a guy out of the front seat, the tout pointed to the open spot.

"Ngapi shillingi?" I asked, confirming the price.

"It is three hundred," the tout responded.

"Are you sure?"

"Only."

Before dishing out the cash, I looked to the back. Maps gave me the thumbs up and I passed dude a 500 shilling note, promptly snatching back two 100 notes before it got swallowed up.

After wedging in between the driver and a rugby-sized Kenyan, I noticed the big man was laughing. Hmmmph, what was so funny? Did I come off like a clown or something? Instinctively, I wanted to call him out, but in circumstances like this, you have to play it safe. Several times in the past, either in East or West Africa, I've spoken to someone who turned out to be a high ranking constable in civilian dress or a village headman camouflaged in shabby clothing. Anyways, before I could make an appraisal, he started talking to me.

"Wewe! You are Mzungu clever. I'm just watching you. Eh, you're checking everything," he said with an every widening grin that exposed a massive set of pearly whites. "Who is sponsoring you?"

"Sasa, I'm just here," I promptly replied, but I was still wondering about his social status. "What is your job?"

"I am a trader."

"Trading what?" I asked, still unsure of his position.

"Just small things."

"Like?" I asked, hoping to get more information.

"You know," he started hesitantly, but smiled big. "There was this calendar of your new President. It showed his whole life, from when he was small boy to President. I got them for ten shillings each. When your people saw them they were so much excited."

"Your people" meant American tourists.

"So, how much did you unload them for?" I asked, knowing someone ended up with the greasy end of the stick.

"They were just liking that calendar," he smiled and forcibly held back a laugh.

"C'mon man, how much?"

As the laughter found a way out, he flashed me the five sign four times and then added, "In your dollars, each."

"You beat them for twenty bucks a pop? No way!"

Trader Big let loose with a deep chuckle that culminated in a Simba sized roar, "I left that place so quickly and did not come back for three days."

Everyone knows this happens, but I was surprised he was giving up the state secrets so freely.

"Ah, you cheated them, bwana," I said while laughing along. "But at least you were eating good."

"Ni kweli!" It's true, he shouted. "I was taking Tusker and nyama big style every night for a whole week!"

As the hours passed, the matatu spun across the picturesque vistas of Taita; a land of rolling plains carpeted with scruffy brush and occasionally broken by inselbergs, massive rocks pushed up from the bowels of the earth.

Buffered by two massive game parks (Tsavo East and West) Voi is at the crossroads of South Eastern Kenya. The Nairobi-Mombasa highway branches off and funnels its way to the Taveta-Holili border crossing with Tanzania. The Lunatic line (the railway to Nairobi) cuts through town and makes a split for Tanzania too. Sisal plantations sprawl across the dips and rises and the Sigalla and Taita Hills break the rolling landscape. Elephants and lions roam the countryside and Somali camel herders are everywhere!

Aside from the game parks the region is also known for gemstones (some of them internationally renowned). Gemstones come from minerals that form three to twenty-five miles deep in the earth's crust. Minerals are naturally occurring substances that have specific physical and chemical compositions.

Rubies, Tomaline, Emeralds and Rhodolite are all found in the area, but the best stones are Tanzanite and Tsavorite. Legend has it a Massai tribesman hauled in a 10,000 carat chunk into a Nairobi jeweler (a carat or (ct) is a 200 milligram unit used for measuring gemstones), but was promptly dismissed as the proprietor thought it only glass. Officially, the stone was discovered in northern Tanzania by a small time prospector named Manuel d'Souza. Again, a Massai comes into play, this time guiding d'Souza to a surface deposit of blue stones in 1967. After heating, Tanzanite is a transparent sapphire-blue stone.

Tsavorite, the other stone of note was also discovered in 1967 by a Scottish geologist named Campbell Bridges. The initial deposits were found in Tanzania, but having difficulties with the government, Bridges went north into Kenya, combing the bush for similar geologic formations and eventually making a second discovery south of Voi in 1971.

Bridges was hard core. He lived in a tree house while battling scorpions, snakes and wild animals. He even played on native superstition and used serpents to guard over his discoveries. Look him up on-line. It's easy to imagine this seasoned adventurer combing through the bush and searching the dry rocky soil for anything of geologic significance once you see his picture. Through hard work and determination Bridges landed the choicest mining claims and built the Scorpion Mine, eventually discovering an 18 carat specimen that was deep forest green in color.

As a result of his efforts, Bridges gained international recognition as a world class gemologist and was also hired as a consultant to a big time jeweler, but his successes didn't sit well with everyone. As a result of these indifferences, the adventurer met his fate in 2009 after being set upon by a savage mob armed with clubs, spears and bow and arrow.

One night on a pub crawl through some of Voi's finer establishments, Maps and I came across some miners, all parties freely voicing their opinion of Campbell Bridges.

"Mr. Bridges was a kind man," a seasoned miner explained to me. "They tried to make it seem like he was having trouble with the locals. That is not true. There are forces that were trying to take away his land. They wanted half of what he built."

But at another venue, Bridges was seen as a tough, brash, and sometimes confrontational.

"How does a man with such money fight with a mob on the roadside?" A man shouted over the din of lively conversations. "He could have just driven away!"

"Ah, he was Zurura!" Another commented vociferously, meaning a guy who profited from the work of others. Regardless of the opinions of Mr. Bridges all parties agreed the outcome was wrong.

Gemstone traders big and small can be found everywhere in Voi. The times I'd been approached in some rickety watering hole are incommensurable, but there are a couple of standouts. Some years ago during one of my previous excursions to Voi, I was enjoying an afternoon cup of chai with a couple of female acquaintances. After reciting the Lord's Prayer, one of them reached into her handbag and produced two small satchels stuffed with dark red and opaque green stones.

"Are you looking for something nice?" she asked, after spilling the samples across a table. The dusty green and red stones looked interesting, but I had no idea what I'd being buying. So, I passed on the deal, but offered to buy another round of chai. Another time, I was approached by a guy on the roadside mumbling something about a "special price" and bearing a collection of dark maroon pebbles in the palm of his hand. I waved him off immediately for fear of some shady deal.

Con jobs aren't only the work of small time traders. In 2009, London's Daily Mail ran a story called the "Curse of the Gem of Tanzania". The article discussed how a bankrupt civil engineering firm had come into possession of a 10,000 carat ruby. The coconut sized stone was said to have been dug up in northern Tanzania near Arusha. The owners even had it appraised at 15 million English Pounds (though the sources were shady). Previously, 2.5 million quid was the most ever paid for a Ruby, there were a lot of questions about its true story. After some careful research and a closer appraisal of the stone, it was determined to be no more than a chunk of angolite (the lowest grade of Ruby).

A year later, the Daily Mail ran another story about the stone. During the engineering company's liquidation process, the ruby was put to auction and sold for 8,000 quid, a far cry from its initial valuation. Despite the drop in value, the new owners hoped to rake in 2 million pounds after the stone is cut and the highest quality rubies could be sold.

Upon reaching Voi's bus stop, we jumped out into the whirling mass of humanity and forged a way to Mapinduzi's ancestral home, one block from the center of town. Drudging up three flights of concrete steps, we landed on the top deck, not only the best view in Voi, but also home to Mama Mapinduzi.

Mama lit up when I entered the sitting room. She became estatic when I presented her with the scarf I'd brought from the States. As we settled in for a cup of chai, Mama called me closer and spoke in low heavy words.

"You have been in Kenya for two weeks and just now getting to Voi. What is happening?"

In very delicate way, I explained there was lady friend in Mombasa who was in need of special counsel.

"Is there a picture?" she asked.

"Yeah, I said," and then retrieved the laptop from my bag of sensitive items and showed her some pictures of Atieno.

Mama started smirking and then gave me a devious look, "Is she a Luo?"

"Yeah," I smiled back.

"Ahhhhhhaaaa-haaaa!" She shouted after seeing Atieno's picture and then smacked me across the thigh with the strength of angry water buffalo goring a lion. "You have too much excitement!"

When Maps older brother arrived, we anted up for a couple of rounds in a local dive.

Before heading out to the bush, I picked Mama up two 1-liter cartons of apple juice. Mama Mapinduzi is almost 80 years old. Physically, she's tired, but mentally she is crisp and alert, which I attribute to her religious consumption of apple juice, she drinks a warm cup every night before going to bed.

XV

Camp Life

By nightfall, we finally reached the schoolhouse. It was pitch black in the bush, save for the sea of stars twinkling overhead. The session had ended and all the school kids were gone. I hunkered down in one of the dorm rooms, making a full appraisal of the accommodations the following day.

Rectangular in form, the cinder block building came with a corrugated roof. Inside, a hallway ran through the middle of the building, just like the keel of a ship, and lots of rooms on either side. There was no running water. We drank from a reservoir filled by runoff from the rains (it tasted great). There was no electricity. So, we read by solar lamp when it was dark and all the cooking was done by fire. The staple was beans and rice, but sometimes the beans came with ugali or chapatti. A couple of times Map's wife whipped up French toast and omelets. Every other day, I sprang for a kilo or two of meat.

Modern plumbing was non-existant, but further along there was a multi-unit outhouse swarming with flies. Showers were served out of a 5-gallon bucket.

Aside from Maps' wife, whom I called Maps kidogo, his teenage kids, a boy and girl, were both home. Maps had an older son who was away at college. There was also a jolly good caretaker who slaughtered chickens at will and never missed a free drink.

At night we all sat around a roaring fire, talking it up until the coals burned out, the conversation swinging wildly from topic-to-topic.

"Ah, we have some real troublemakers this time," Maps sounded off and complained about the student body. "I've already notified the parents. Don't send them back."

"We don't need them," Maps kidogo reiterated with the authority of a tested school administrator. "No matter how many millions of Tanzanian shillings they bring. They can just keep it."

The caretaker talked about how a mob of Somali brigands hacked eight Taita to death over livestock grazing.

"You see," he started angrily. "These Somalis are pushing the camel onto people's land and destroy the soil."

"That camel urine is very acidic," Maps added. "It's some time before crops will grow again.

As a result of the digressions, a group of farmers confronted the Somali herders. Rightfully so, since these brigands were operating in complete disregard to property rights, but it ended badly.

"Eiee, those Somalis," Maps' daughter said. "They just whistle and so many come from the bushes. You don't know how many are out there."

"What did the police do," I asked, while envisioning eight bloody bodies sprawled out on the rocky soil.

"Nothing," Maps responded bluntly and then shook his head. "This is a big deal, Eric. They say the camels are already sold to someone in Saudi Arabia and top guys are taking money on this side for grazing rights."

"Ehhh," the old man grunted and then threw his hands up in the air.

After a break in the conversation, Maps daughter started speaking again. "Why is the Illuminati so strong in America?"

"What?"

"The Illuminati?" Maps' son spoke for the first time. "Everyone who is big in America must be a member of the Illuminati."

Maps daughter recited a list of popular entertainers and a few well known politicians. "Even the president must be Illuminati or he will not be made president of America."

When pressed, Maps indicated they got it from school and that it is pervasive in Kenya's social-cultural milieu. "Most believe it is a secret society that rules the world."

Surprisingly, this was the second time someone had mentioned the Illuminati while I was in Kenya. One night during a lull in the activities, Atieno went into a monologue about the Illuminati. She was absolutely convinced America's youth were joining this secret society in droves and even offered to retrieve a documentary from a friend. In fact, the way she spoke, you'd think they had their tentacles stretched across the country and strangling the nation.

After explaining that I wasn't so sure about the Illuminati, I advised Map's kids to watch out for the Bilderburg Group and the Federal Reserve Bank. "They're the real troublemakers."

A few days later, the sound of loud music reverberated up from a village on the main road. So, Maps and I ventured off on a recon mission. A massive crowd had gathered around a couple of tents where a celebration was planned for a local woman who had made well. Some clever talking and my Mzungu status got us seated in the VIP section where we were promptly served a plate of chicken pilau and bottle of water. I didn't have the stomach to wait out the festivities. So, after scarfing down the grub, it was time to move.

"Look," I said to my esteemed associate. "I'm gonna walk over to the those bushes and tap a kidney. When I'm out of view, break for the road, ok?"

Maps nodded his head and fifteen minutes later, we were at local shack knocking down our first round for the day and planning our next objective.

XVI

The Spirits of Taita

Wundanyi, a hilltop enclave, was the drop point. The run up was straight and level until we ascended into the Taiti Hills, a cluster of granite slabs piled up like smashed dominos. I don't know why they called them hills, because they looked more like little mountains. Edging along, the matatu creaked and groaned its way up and around a pot-holed road, occasionally gassing out the stank of an overworked transmission. Carved into the face of the hill, the road gave the driver little room for error; at times the narrow shoulder yielding to a one hundred foot drop. Wrecks were not uncommon. In fact, Maps had once been victim of vehicular unpleasentries. One time on the down swing, the transmission gave out on a Matatu. Luckily, it only slammed into a rock wall and then flipped over into a ditch. Despite having a compressed neck, Maps most vivid memory were the thieves working him over as he wrestled his way free of the vehicle.

Rugged hills and granite faced cliffs formed up as we gained altitude. The slopes were terraced out and small square homes were crammed into the largest plots. Halfway up the air turned refreshingly cool and the vegetation changed to lush, green and leafy.

Maps and I jumped out in the middle of town and took to a path that led to higher ground. Wading through a patch of thorn bushes we came to a craggy rock overhang, but it was empty; no skulls or anything to indicate a shrine.

"Ask that kid," I said, pointing back down into the dip.

Maps yelled in Taita and the kid raced in our direction.

"He says there's another cave further up. What do you think, buddy?"

"Why not, we're here."

The boy guided us up a steep-but-worn path criss-crossed with tree roots. We high stepped our way up and held on to the roots for balance. My thighs burned and I huffed-and-puffed heavily. Maps kept asking what was wrong and the kid smirked every time he looked back at me.

Fifteen minutes later we'd scaled the incline. At the top, we marched over another hilltop before reaching the summit and then worked our way down several large boulders to a large split in the stone. A steady stream of water disappeared into the gap.

"Take care, brother," Maps said, and then pointed down at the surface of the rock. It was wet and there was a thin film of moss. "This place is dangerous."

"The view is hellacious," I said. "But the cave is a wild goose chase."

"He's saying it's too slippery to see right now."

"Then ask him where the skulls are."

The two chattered back and forth and the youth pointed back down the hill (great).

Off we went, cascading along washed out paths and then plunging into three foot deep gouges that fanned out for a few strides on level ground before plunging down again. Finally, the ground leveled out and we rolled up on the back side of a rock overhang.

There was a caretaker nearby. So, our guide ran off to inform him we'd arrive. The kid came back and said he wasn't home, but it was ok to visit, and then signaled for us to proceed. Creeping under the rock, we angled to the left and found the first shrine. Topside, five skull caps were lined up against the rock. In the crevice below were the fractured remains of several skulls and an empty cast iron pot. Further down in the rough, there was a better set of specimens. In the confines of a narrow rock shelf, seven skulls stared straight out. Minus the lower mandible, they were all in good shape. One distinguished by a layer of green moss completely covering its face.

"What do you think, buddy?" Maps asked.

I had grand visions on the way up; caves illuminated by dozens of candles and the air saturated by twirling wisps of smoke. and generations of skulls layered up so densely the oldest specimens were fused together through the same process that creates stalactites and stalagmites.

"I think there is a larger site further up in the hills, but that's two more hours away," Maps acknowledged. "It might still be a sacred. So, there'd be a lot of rituals to perform when visiting. In fact, they might not even allow you to visit."

Since the caretaker was gone, I couldn't get the full picture on the site or what might be found deeper in the hills. However, back on the coast, I spoke with another Taita man who confirmed there was a much larger cave with generations of skulls kept there.

After a couple of more days at the camp, I was back in Port Reitz, just missing the action! There were thirty-five chickens of all sizes and age in Atieno's chicken coop; she was well versed in their language. One night, when they started up in a disturbed kind of way, she went out to see what was going on. The preliminary examination revealed nothing, but on the second venture into the coup, she discovered a 6 foot cobra. The thing had bitten 5 of the smaller chickens and the only reason she didn't get zapped was because the snake had one stuck in its mouth. Upon seeing this, Atieno screamed so loud that the masai watchmen came down and whacked it over the head and then burned the body just in case it was carrying babies.

XVII

The City of Graves

Rejuvenated by Taita's cooler climate I took to the road again, this time heading towards North Coast. Once free from the clutches of Mombasa, the driver put his foot down and we rocketed north on the coast highway. Jumping out at the junction just before the Kilifi Bridge, I worked my way through dusty lanes and past ramshackle stalls until finding the sign that pointed to the ruins. At the gate, I was promptly harpooned for 500 Kenyan Shillings.

"This price includes a visitation to the reptile park," the gateman smiled, in an attempt to soften the blow.

"Who gives a flying catamaran?" I said while grimacing over the cost of entry. "The only time I want to see snakes is before they attack. Where are the ruins?"

Still smiling, he pointed to a sandy path that led up to a staircase marked as having 104 steps.

There are several parts to Mnarani ruins: bulky chunks of a great mosque, and the fractured remains of a small mosque. The balance of the assignment is on a wooded hill overlooking the Kilifi river. Most notable is a large, fluted column rising up from the main mosque.

Figuring there was more to the site I veered off the path and wrestled through a tangle of vines. Sure enough, not more than fifteen feet off the trail were the remains of a long building; the top of the walls poking above the layers of dirt, twigs and leaves. On the other side of the path, the fractured remains of something formidable was being consumed by the jungle.

Mnarani is reminiscent of other ruins along the North Coast, though on a much smaller scale. Years ago I visited several other sites much larger in scope. First there's the "Lost City of Gedi" and second, the ruins of Pate Island.

Crack open an atlas and check the north coast on a map of Kenya. You'll find a black square with three white dots stacked up in a triangle at the Watamu junction. Gedi is a major site, but little is known of its origins. History books say it was founded in the late 13th century. It's possible the city's roots lay further back with an unknown race of seafaring people. A wide variety of artifacts unearthed onsite indicates Gedi was once a port on the Indian Ocean and the inhabitants enjoyed a prosperous lifestyle. Today, it sits five kilometers back from the Indian Ocean.

Sometime during the 16th century Gedi suffered from rapid depopulation brought on by the advance of the Galla. They were a murderous lot who swept south from Somalia and laid siege to everything in their path. The lasting legacy of these brigands lay in the city's name. The word "Gedi" is Galla for precious. This renaming could be a reference to the acquisition of treasure or other valuable commodities. After the looting, several decades passed before the city received an influx of new inhabitants; possibly displaced coastal peoples who built mosques and modified existing structures with Islamic designs.

For the most part, the city seems to have existed in relative obscurity. Portuguese adventurers make no mention of the place. Arab colonizers seemed to have overlooked it, too. It wasn't until 1884 that the site received a formal visit. John Kirks, a British official from Zanzibar, led a small expedition to the ruins. Afterwards, the site drifted back into anonymity until the early 20th century when a restoration effort began. By the late 1940's Gedi had been established as a National Park.

The site covers forty-five acres and is ringed by two different walls. Broken and crumbling, the main ruins have endured so much erosion the coral rag blocks used in construction are now exposed. Any finished surfaces left are stained, faded or tainted green by a veneer of jungle moss. Much of the original stone town has been reduced to a jagged outline in the ground, but a couple of buildings stand out. The tight compartments and high walls of the Grand Mosque and the Palace retain a sense of the once overwhelming architecture.

Of the entire site, only twelve acres have been dug up and cleared. This leaves a lot of room for exploration. The best way to get started is by striking out on one of the muddy tracks that loop through the forest. The best time to visit is during the rainy season, it's nice and steamy and the foliage is in full gear.

Within a few feet, the vegetation closes in overhead and encapsulates the trail. You'd think the shade would ease the humidity, but it only gets worse. It's like a steam house and each step is measured by the buckets of perspiration leaking out of your body.

Just wipe that sweat off your brow and keep slogging forward, because in a few more strides you'll be pushing aside low hanging branches and picking through the empty shell of an abandoned structure. Further along you'll skirt the fractured remains of the city's outer wall, stopping every few feet to peer deeper into the shadowy spots between the leaves and tree trunks.

Back in the rough, a haunting silence hangs in the air, occasionally broken by monkeys thrashing overhead. The distraction is momentary. Soon you'll be back to dreaming about big pots of gold and piles of exotic gem stones, but take care. The property is peppered with deep wells. One bad step and your little expedition will come to a bone splintering halt.

Eventually, the trail leads back into the main settlement. By then it's time for a breather. Take a few minutes and squat down within the Great Mosque or the Palace Courts. Listen closely, with a little imagination the electric buzz of clattering insects becomes the voices of long dead inhabitants. Laborers wrestle with the day's work and shopkeepers haggle with bargain hunters. As the sun dips and the sea breeze rustles through the treetops, veiled women of questionable repute push their wares. Sailors crowd dingy cafes, sip spiced tea and spin yarns about sea monsters and mermaids. Hell, you might even catch Captain Sinbad boasting about his conquests on some torrid island.

Yes, Gedi is a mysterious place. Although the architecture suggests an Islamic influence, no one is sure of its origins. However, its role as a port city is certain. The lingering question is, how did it become landlocked? You'll have to go back to the map book and review the section on plate tectonics. Quite likely, the region endured a geologic event of titanic proportions, thrusting the Earth's crust upward and causing the Ocean waters to drain away.

Before we move on, it should be noted that lost cities aren't the only sites of archaeological interest Kenya has to offer. In issue 46 of Msafiri (Kenya Airways in-flight magazine) there was an article written by Daniel Stiles called "The Azanian Civilization Revisited". In the essay, Stiles writes about excavating ancient graves in the arid reaches of Kenya's extreme north. Through extensive surveying, he indentified the existence of hundreds of stone rings in the Marsabit District. These graves, 17 meters in diameter and 1 meter high, often yielded skeletons in excess of 6 feet tall. It is believed that these were constructed by a race of "ancient giants from the East African interior who constructed colossal stone monuments". The works of this lost race can also be found in southern Ethiopia and Somalia.

Through research conducted in the 1950s, they were named Megalithic Cushites. However, it is believed these people were the red skinned "giants" mentioned in the ancient navigator book called the "Periplus of the Erythrean Sea" when describing the peoples of Azania (the coast from Somalia to Mozambique). In the article, Stiles final assessment of these peoples is that they were absorbed by the Bantu and Islamic migrations that overtook the region.

Back on the main drag, I caught a matatu southbound and then ditched out at Mtwapa; a bustling joint just up from Mombasa. Mobs of people swirled around on both sides of the road like organisms multiplying under a microscope slide. Matatus landed on the muddy flats between the shops and the road, disgorging their victims or taking on new fodder, and pods of boda-bodas idled all over the place.

Because the day was drawing to an end, I had to work over a boda-boda brigand as quickly as possible. Holding up a crisp fifty shilling note by its mid-section, I began flapping the bill up and down like it had wings.

"Angalia ndege kidogo, kaka?" Brother, do you see the little bird? I asked in Swahili. "He's gonna fly away if you don't act fast. Haraka! Haraka! Get it?"

"Eti?"

"Na sema. If you don't take this nini, I'm gonna find a guy who will. So, are we doing business or what?"

Normally, this is the point when they start whining about the cost of petrol, but dude just smirked.

"For that small money, you can drive me," he lightly chuckled.

Oh, so he's gonna call my bluff, eh?

"You got it, pal!" I snapped back, and then went to push him back on his own bike.

Still amused, he slapped my hand away and signaled me to jump on the back.

"Kuenda!" We go, he said.

Revving up his bike, we ran through the human meat grinder and then angled off the tarmac and onto a sandy path. It was so dusty, the bike fish tailed every time he shifted gears, but that only added to his story. You see, before entering the highly competitive world of boda-boda drivers, he had a different job all together; this guy used to work as a casual at a big hotel.

"Do you know what that is?" Paul asked, after introducing himself.

"Yeah, it means your future is uncertain."

"Yes, that's true," he laughed, and then further elaborated on the job. "A casual makes sure the visitors are enjoying themselves. At the hotel, I played ping pong with the guests. I even beat the Chinese man, but I have to let the guests win most of the time or I won't see tips.

"Eh, I had so many friends at the place. The guests were always asking me to come eat with them. So, I'm taking breakfast, lunch and even dinner with many Mzungu," he reminisced jovially. "I made small money, only 400 shillings per day, but there were many tips. I saved them. After sometime, I bought this motorbike."

"So, what's a good day on the bike then?"

"Eight hundred shillings can be a small day, but sometimes I can make two thousand or more. It depends."

Cutting through a field of thinly planted maize, we landed on a dirt road and then cruised into the ruins. Before Paul cut out, I slide him a pen and paper and got his mobile number. He'd come in handy for the ride back. Quick witted, Paul worked it to the very end.

"So, this is when I write down my PIN number, right?"

A-hah-hah, the laughter, the laughter!

Jumba la Mtwana is a large site nestled right next to the Oceanside; there's a significant amount of structures still standing. If you get there, I'd suggest blowing off the museum and jumping right into the thick of it; the museum is only one room and you can catch it on the way out.

It's best to start in a southern direction. After passing through the breach in a low wall you'll find the largest structures on your left. Although they're crumbling away, at some point in the past they were multi-storied. Guiding through the arched doorways and peeking into the guts of the joint, you'll notice many small rooms. The windowless compartments will have you wondering what their function was: storeroom or dungeons?

Continue flanking along the southern side of the site. You'll pass along narrow passages and through the fractured shells of this once thriving town. Drifting wide past a massive baobab tree you'll find a collection of debris piles. After counting them up, hook back to your left. There, you'll see the path that takes you down a flight of steps to the beach. If your timing is good, you might catch a handful of locals burning incense in the old mosque, but the rhythmic sounds of waves rolling onto the beach and the gust of an afternoon sea breeze is even better. After enjoying yourself, wander across the sand and end up in the house of the rounded wall.

At this point, you have a choice to make. Do you get packed to the gills with the fresh fish and the spicy prawns they're grilling at the seaside joint, or do you keep pushing on? For me, it was an easy decision. I chugged back my last swig of water, finished a sleeve of ginger snap cookies and then headed back into the ruins.

There's a two meter high wall on the right running all the way back to the museum. At the beginning it's completely disheveled, but it gets back to good form until the section where the Swahili god of thunder bit a chunk out of it. You can take the smooth side walk like you're strolling through the park, but if you want a bit of edge to it, head back into the rough. There's a nice little surprise waiting there. Do you want to know where it is? Well, I'm not telling. You can stumble on it all on your own.

So, just mind how you round out on those shells, friend. Before you know it you're going to walk up on that pit (an old well). Just over a yard in width, that thing plummets into the darkness and it's only safety provisions are a few strands of barb wire that the last guy dragged down with him.

Before heading out, I grabbed another view of the place. The way the standing masonry is broken up and tilts to the sides, it looks like an abandoned cemetery. As the sun dipped in the west, its final rays filtered through the foliage and illuminated the ruins with an eerie glow. Soon, it would fade into twilight and then the spirits of the dead would swirl amongst the ruins.

By now the Ethiopian section of my trip was nearly written up, but I was losing sight of the objective (traveling all the way down to South Africa). For a couple of days I'd contemplated camping out in Kenya for the duration; who could blame me?

Every morning Atieno prepared tea mixed with milk and laced with ginger. For lunch, she cut up a big bowl of fruit fresh from the market. If she didn't cook dinner we went to an outdoor establishment called Apollo for big plates of nyama choma and ugali, and, every night she made sure I had plenty of dessert.

Life had gotten easy. I had only planned on staying in Kenya for two weeks. The third had blown by before I even realized it and I was half way through the fourth when it dawned on me. So one night, well after the sun went down, I told Atieno it was time to resume my journey. At first she began to fidget and then clung to me tightly, I thought I might not get away, but by the next morning she agreed.

"So, when will you come back?" she asked in a somber way.

"Soon," I replied.

"When is soon?" She said sharply.

"Soooooooooon."

Tanzania: Intercession

XVIII

The City of Dung

Two days later Atieno and I made an early morning run into Mombasa. I had a seven o'clock ticket for the ride to Dar es Salaam. After reaching Tanzania's capitol city, I would resume my observations in archaeology further down the coast.

Atieno lectured the driver on his responsibilities and my well being and then I boarded the bus. Luckily I had a window seat on the sidewalk side, keeping my eyes on her and waving good bye until the bus pulled away. It was a massive metal box with a blue velvet interior. Two columns of two seats each ran along either side of the interior and sliver like luggage racks were overhead. A skinny aisle ran down the middle like a spine. You could stash your kit in the cargo holds down below, but if you did you'd be rubber necking at every stop, making sure no one was siphoning off your gear.

At roughly 7:30 am the leviathan pulled away from the curb and then growled through the gritty streets of Mombasa. Before we could really get rolling there was the Likoni ferry to contend with; a battered and rusty motorized barge that linked the island with the south coast. Vehicles of all sorts filled the lower deck. People were relegated along the sides of the vessel. All passengers had to alight from the bus and ride in the ferry's pedestrian section; a pick pocket's playground where passengers are herded together like livestock. I've had my fair share of crossings in the past, so there was no reason to fight my way through that mess again. I was staying onboard the leviathan. When the conductor said everyone had to get off, I told him I was tired.

"But you must exit the bus," he protested.

"Uh ah," I replied, and then flipped him a forty bob Shilling coin. "Get it?"

"Sawa, sawa," He smiled, indicating everything was cool, but also signaling for me to close the window curtains. "So, polisi can't see."

After the crossing, the driver raced south and reached the border in just under an hour. Getting stamped by immigrations on each side of the border and changing money (one thousand Kenyan shillings got nineteen thousand Tanzanian shillings) took another hour. Soon after loading back up, we were sailing south along a narrow two lane road at incredible rates of speed, halting at police check points and slowing for the occasional highway smash up. Since nothing notable happened along the way to Dar, I'm going to give you the low down on the Swahili (I was having so much fun in Kenya, I forgot about it).

As defined by James S. Kirkman, a prominent Kenyan archaeologist, the region known as the Swahili Coast begins in southern Somalia and stretches all the way down to the northern fringes of Mozambique, comprising nearly two thirds of East Africa, snaring the islands of Zanzibar, Pemba and Mafia along the way. The earliest mariners gave reports of giant red-haired savages, a race of people who've been lost to the fog of time. However, through field research, it is known that Bushmen, those curious chaps who track across parts most inhospitable, originally inhabited the region, at least until being pushed south by the Bantu. Over a thousand years ago Arab and Persian traders, adventurers and those subject to political persecution loaded upon dhows and rode the monsoons south (they blow southwest Nov-April and northeast May-Oct).

Dhows are traditional sailboats that originated from southern Arabia. They come in several sizes (the smallest being one of the most common sites along the East African seaboard) and have earned their keep through the centuries, hauling crew and cargo as far south as Mozambique and as far east as India and China. They are made from hand tooled wood. The largest are held together by hundreds of miles of coir (rope made from coconut fiber) and then swabbed over with vegetable oil to become water proof. It is said that the best assembled ships could last one hundred years.

Gliding along the swells of the Indian Ocean, they landed on coral islands and along the sandy shores of the palm fringed coast. Coral is a marine invertebrate typically found in shallow tropical waters. They grow in colonies and produce calcium carbonate based exoskeletons. Bits and pieces of the exoskeleton break off and accumulate with other aqua-marine materials to form a reef.

Most of these mariners were men. So, as being starved by the sea, they took in with local Bantu women and through their native mingling, the Swahili people were born and their communities began to dot the coast.

Blocks of coral rag were stacked and finished with lime, forming towns and cities that traded far and near across the Indian Ocean basin. At first, they bartered with elephant tusks, slaves and gold with traders in the Middle-East, India, China and the Spice Islands. To this day, Chinese porcelain can be found embedded in tombs along the coast (fragments speckle the ground at some ruins). In return, they brought in iron implements, stoneware, silks and spices. Careful research has determined that a skilled trader journeying to the Swahili coast could generate enough profit that would last him a life time. Early on cowrie shells (small rounded shells that are porcelain-like in appearance) were used as currency until the most powerful settlements minted their own coinage.

Through these oceanic interactions, the Chinese arrived in the Lamu archipelago in massive ships. Their stay was brief. Next, wave-after-wave of Portuguese fleets rounded the Cape of Good

Hope and then headed north. Grand adventurers like Vasco de Gama, Pedro Alvares Cabral, and Ruy Lourenco Ravasco visited almost every settlement they found. If a tribute of gold could not be extracted the Swahili were set upon (Malindi got smart and dealt with the Portuguese on friendly terms). Buildings were burned to the ground, towns people slaughtered, women subjected to uncivilized discourse and anything that wasn't nailed to the floor, was rounded up, carted off and then packed aboard ship.

After the Portuguese reign, the coast was subjected to marauding natives (who made the Portuguese look like amateurs) and European rivalries. At the Berlin conference in 1894, the Swahili Coast was sectioned and quartered into spheres of influence; Italy in the north, the British and Germans administering the central part and the southern balance yielded to Portugal. As a result of World War I and the Winds of Change (the era of African independence), Swahili-land is now divided between Somalia, Kenya, Tanzania and northern Mozambique. In recent times there have been outbursts about Kenya's coastal region regarding independence, though the discussion is not taken seriously.

Kiswahili, the language of the people, is spoken purely along the coast. It's the national language of Tanzania, the lingua franca of Kenya and heard as deep as the Congo. It has its own dialect in the Comoros Archipelago(a group of islands in the Indian Ocean). It's easy to learn and mandatory when slumming in East Africa. With a little practice you'll easily come up with some key phrases that help outmaneuver corrupt shop owners and fraudulent taxi drivers.

Through the centuries, the Swahili style remains unchanged. To this day, men still sport a kikoy (a cloth worn about the waist) and don a kanzu (a tight fitting hat; the sharpest being white). Women, who are true believers, will be dressed in black head to toe (called ninja style). The most ardent wearing socks and gloves; only their eyes are known.

Through the years, their food has been refined. Keep a look out for the "Swahili Dishes" sign. My favorite is Chicken Biryani. Whether it's scooped from a bucket at a roadside shack or served upon the trappings of a respectable diner, it's one of the finest dishes. Sure there's other stuff, like pilau, but nothing compares to spicy tomato sauce and chunks of chicken served over coconut rice.

As a result of this rich history, the coast and islands of East Africa are dotted by ruined stone settlements. The largest are maintained as parks and historic sites, but smaller ones are still shrouded by the green tangle of coastal vegetation. There's even a story of a sunken city. Years ago on a brief excursion to Pemba Island (Zanzibar's northern sister) I was informed by a dive master about a small island that had been stacked so high the land mass could not support the weight of the buildings set upon it.

To get a solid understanding of the coastal ruins, read Kirkman's "Men and Monuments on the East African Coast". Although a bit dated (it was first published in 1964) the book gives a run down on all things archaeology. Kirkman even dives into the Comoros and Madagascar, discussing the lasting effects of Swahili and European material culture.

Ten hours later, we pulled into Dar es Salaam. It was hot, humid and the sun's final rays were dancing along the horizon.

Rolling into an unknown destination at night is a worst case scenario for any traveler. The possibilities of getting mugged, misled, or molested is at its highest point. By sundown, in cities far and near, most decent people have called it a day and the animals are prowling the streets in greater numbers. It didn't take long for my mzungu status to shine through like a beacon. Inadvertently, I got to jawing about places to stay with a half-backed chap, who, by the smell of things, spent a lot of time sleeping in the park.

"Twenty thousand shillings is the limit, pal," I said, thinking it would shake him off.

"No problem, rafiki," he replied, and then retrieved a worn hotel brochure from his back pocket.

"Twenty thousand only," he stated, and then jabbed his grimy mitt at the name on the paper, Dai City Palace.

"OK, where's the place at?" I asked from a safe distance, his stench was overwhelming.

"Just a few minute's walk from here, rafiki," he said with assurance, and then signaled up a side street with sporadic car and boda-boda (motorcycle) traffic.

Now, I don't normally advise pursuing this course of action, it's only that my back was up against the wall and the longer, safer, route would have cost more. So, with both bags firmly shouldered, I followed his lead up the darkened street, constantly looking from side-to-side and checking the alleys, glancing to the rear for that odd street goon or sly motorcycle driver who thought he could beat me from the blind spot. Whenever we passed a group of people I scrutinized them surreptitiously from the corner of my eye. Did they break from their conversations and size me up in a bad way? Did someone stand up and follow me? Luckily, I was only victim to a few inquisitive looks.

A few blocks later we found the hotel just off the junction of Mafia and Congo streets. The section of town was known as Kariakoo, a densely built up area where multistory concrete buildings were wedged in together like dominos. Street vendors cooked food in big vats of grease, people conversed loudly and watery substances stained the streets with dark patches.

Per night, rooms were closer to thirty thousand, but after a bit of haggling, the front desk clerk let one go for twenty-five. To make amends, she tossed in a breakfast. Content with the arrangement, I threw the bum a dash and then hustled upstairs.

Man, this place was choice. First off, the room smelled like it been dredged up from the bottom of a river. Second, I bagged two cock roaches right after dropping my bags (one was pretty meaty too). Third, the room's mirror was spider webbed like it had got jacked during a drunken man's rage, but best of all, the mineral build up on the bathroom fixtures was the size of whale barnacles.

After replenishing my stock of water and snacks from a nearby duka (small shop), I retired for the evening, sleeping with the light on in fear of what might come creeping out in the dark.

Breakfast was served from the hole-in-the-wall next store. The chai was spot on and the eggs and toast came with a rat hair, but that was nothing. Remember those leaky spots in the street I was talking about? Well, just after sitting down at a table I caught a whiff of raw sewage. It was light, hardly fleeting, yet there. At first I didn't think much about it, other than watching my step when I was out in the street. But as more and more cars sped by and the sticky sound of tires running over moist asphalt gained prominence, I began wondering. Surely the tires were kicking up aerosols that whirled around in the air and landed all over. Was it possible that cholera could be transmitted that way? Africans have a saying "people can just die", meaning someone has acquired a sickness and passed on. Somewhat unnerved, I pushed away my half eaten breakfast and got to the order of business.

Nestled in mid-way along Tanzania's coast, Dar es Salaam (the Haven of Peace) was established in the 1860's by a slave trader called Sayyid Majid bin Said Al Busaid. The town floundered until the arrival of the German's in 1887. Under their Teutonic tutelage a foundation for commerce and governance was laid and topped up with some mighty fine architectural specimens(look up some old time pix of the Governor's Mansion and the Ocean Road Hospital).

After a bit of a row, the Brits ousted the Germans in 1919 and held court until the Winds of Change. Since then, Dar has been on her own; an Afro-Arab mix with all things Indian Ocean. Today she is the pulse of the nation, one of the fastest growing cities on the continent, and one of the largest ports on Africa's eastern seaboard. Dar is also the hub for a mesh of roads and railways that link the country and reach many points further in the interior of the continent.

After converting a few one hundred dollar bills into a fat roll of Tanzanian Shillings, I hopped a bus speckled with faded Chinese characters and headed to Bagara Transit Station. Packed to the gills, the medium-sized bus was stifling inside. I was leaking everywhere and my clothes were blotched with heavy wet spots.

"Are you okay?" a fellow commuter asked, as I smeared the river of sweat off of my temple.

"The humidity is killing me, man," I replied.

Thankfully, a kind soul offered up his window seat so I could breathe again.

With the rainy season in full swing, slosh was pooled up everywhere at Bagara. You could sense the cholera, dysentery, and who knows what else lurking in the murky water. Shredded plastic, drink containers, bones, fabrics and metal parts were embedded in the damp soil. Every time something gritty crunched between my teeth I spit feverishly, as a cautionary measure.

By mid-morning, the Kilwa bus had already filled up. I tried to bargain my way on African style, but, surprisingly got nowhere.

"Buy now for tomorrow's 5:30 bus," a tall man advised, but wasting another day in Dar was out of the question. I had to keep moving. Glancing at a rough map I'd sketched out, I asked about the towns that came before Masoka. If I could get close enough, the end run would just be a local taxi.

"What about Moholo or Nangurukuru," I asked. "Can I get a bus there today?

"No," he replied adamantly.

"No?" I echoed skeptically. "Are you sure?"

"Maybe try Ubungo."

Ubongo was another hell hole that handled longer trips. Slogging back through the grimy lot, I angled for the main road, but was intersected by a portly fellow with a big ball cap and an even bigger mouth.

"Moholo! Moholo!" He shouted, with big white eyes.

"What?" I exclaimed, thinking that I'd been tripped up by a mirage.

"Where do you go?" He smiled broadly.

"Moholo."

"Get in!" He commanded, and then pointed towards a stout bus with large glass windows.

Unreal! I hadn't gone more than fifty feet from the no-can-do ticket office and rounded up a ride to Moholo. This was absolutely astonishing. In Kenya, the touts would have slugged it out to get mzungu on the right bus (that's how they get the money). Here, I had to find it on my own.

Thirty minutes later we were southbound, swaying gently from side-to-side, as the driver gunned it down a narrow highway. There was no shoulder on this road. The highs were enclosed by embankments and the lows gave way to soggy green fields, but the driver didn't care. Heavy rains and a fogged up windshield was no reason to exercise caution. He only braked after being flagged by the traffic police.

Four hours later, my fat buddy started up again. "Moholo, rafiki! Moholo!"

"This is it?"

"Yes! Yes! Yes!" His head bobbed up and down.

"Shit!" I expostulated unintentionally and a series of muffled laughs reverberated through the bus.

In less than twenty-four hours a second worst case scenario unfolded; this time being dropped off in the middle of nowhere with no prospects of further transportation.

"Don't worry," one of the passengers chuckled. "Another bus is coming."

As the Moholo bus veered off down a muddy track, I made a quick glance up and down the road. There was nothing there except a handful of small shops selling basic food stuffs, drinks, vegetables and stinky fish. A few idlers camped out in the shady spots, but it didn't take long for the weirdoes to materialize. Within minutes a group of desperate-looking fellows gathered around and started pointing at their mouths and rubbing their stomachs. Heck, I couldn't tell if they were going to rob me or eat me. Hoping to defer any belligerent actions, I made simple conversation with them, but it did nothing to alleviate the hungry look in their eyes. Luckily, another leviathan arrived before they got the fires going under a giant pot. Can you believe that it was the same bus that was "filled up" at Bagara Terminal?

As soon as the door opened, I elbowed my way onto the over-stuffed transport, edging out a couple of market women for the last spot. No sooner did I breathe a sigh of relief then there was an abrupt tugging on my right side. Looking down, I spotted a brown hand fingering its way into my pocket. Through the confusion of people mobbing the doorway, one of the vagrants was trying to steal my dough!

"Hey!" I shouted, and then jammed a Bic Pen into the fleshy part between his knuckles. All hell broke loose and the hand recoiled away amid a cackle of hoots and hollers. Capitalizing on the disturbance, the driver closed the door, boxing out the madness so we could get back on the road.

Tired, grimy and miserable, I'd flunked the diligence test, but after a quick survey discovered my cash, the equivalent of thirty bucks US, was still wedged in the bottom of my pocket (Whew, that was close!).

Crammed into the stairwell with my back pressed against an unsecured door of a rapidly moving vehicle, I was on my way. My bag of sensitive items pinched up precariously between my knees. There was no fidget room whatsoever and the sweat was cascading down my face, washing across my back and dripping off my knee caps. Staying dry was going to be a real trick. When the bus was at full speed it wasn't bad. A steady rush of air blew across my face, but when the bus slowed for road work, which was a lot, I got roasted.

As time passed by the passengers thinned out and I was able to find a level of comfort. First securing a sitting spot in the stairwell, then graduating to a three legged stool in the aisle at the front before having a bench seat to myself.

"Mzungu, how do you like?" Someone shouted while I was squatted on the stool precariously above the driver's left side.

"I'm riding shotgun now, pal!" I roared; the driver and some of the passengers joining in for a laugh.

When the bus stopped, the driver called me over to his side. I thought he might have some information on a local guest house, but instead, he made a peculiar request.

"Those shoes," he said nonchalantly and then pointed down at the pair of blue Gilligan's Islands I'd snagged off the clearance rack at an Old Navy. "Can I have them?"

"They are the only shoes I have," I laughed, slightly taken aback by his request.

XIX

Kilwa Masoka

Just down the road from the terminus, I found a stuffy little hole called the New Mjaka Enterprises Guest House. A curious fellow called Brother James (more on him later) directed me there. Fifteen thousand shillings got a "banda" for the night; essentially a hut of modern trappings divided into three sections, a sitting room, bedroom and wash room. Running water was a problem, but I'll spare you the details on the lavatory. The bed was in the middle of the room, a worn mosquito net hung from a wooden rectangle mounted from the ceiling and the fan spun right above it.

Masoka town is spread out across a flat peninsula. There's an assortment of small shops, restaurants and other businesses ratcheted in together around the bus stop (some of them outfitted with air conditioning units). All the food joints kept a glass box quarter filled with French fries and a tray of eggs stacked on top. The main road runs straight down to the port. All points in the town are interconnected by a mesh of sandy tracks and foot paths. The population was young and I rarely saw any other mzungu while there.

It was hot and the air was so saturated you had to tunnel through the humidity with a knife. Every time I cleaned up and put on fresh clothes, I went sweat ball in a minutes, putting my nice tropical linens in a soggy mood. Running the fan full blast seemed like the best way to beat it, but all it did was swish the humidity around and give me a nasty head cold that lasted for the duration of my stay.

Mosquitoes breached the wire every evening and tore me to shreds. At night there were torrential downpours that stopped as suddenly as they started. Every morning Brother James came by at 7 am sharp.

"Yo, G! What are you doing?"

"I'm sleeping. What do you think I'm doing?"

The first order of business was to meet with the antiquities officer and secure a visitation permit for Kilwa Kisiwani. It cost 27,000 TZ shillings (talk about steep!), but it gets worse. By law you have to hire an official guide. That cost 15,000 shillings more. Then you have to organize transport on a local boat, that's another 10,000, but (get this) the locals only pay 500 TZ! These were all official rates sanctioned by the Tanzanian Government.

This is where the Honorable Mwalimu Brother James Mchokozi, English teacher at large and Football Mercenary abroad, comes into play.

Brother James had a stocky frame, bald black head and very alert eyes. His attire consisted of African football jerseys and black running shorts. One day, Brother James arrived wearing a pair of heavy framed glasses. The style suited him well. So, I told him.

"Hey bro, you look like a professor, mwalimu kubwa!" The big teacher, I said. James wore the glasses everyday from then on.

His command of English was blunt and peppered with phrases like, "G", "Yo-yo-yo!", and "Bro, waddup".

James knew the town inside and out and hanging with the guy paid dividends. Like when acquiring mosquito coils; I'd gone to half a dozen shops and come up empty handed. James walked us over to the pocket and scored a box the first time. When I mistakenly mixed up my stash of good batteries with the expired ones, he knew who would test out the duds for free. James also had the pesky habit of inserting himself into the middle of everything. For instance, he would snatch the money from my hand and then give it to the shopkeeper. Then, he would intercept the merchandise and look it over before passing it to me, every single time. Ahh, I needed a guide, not a handler!

In a previous life, Brother James made the rounds in Dar es Salaam and collected used motor oil for resale.

"Maybe you can get 20 liter for 4,000 shillings and then resell for 6,000," he reminisced with a slight smile. "Sometimes you get lucky and find a 45 gallon drum, but it's hard, bro. There are so many guys doing that job."

Hoping for better fortunes, James traveled to South Africa for "small business" and ended up playing minor league football, but the gig was temporary.

"One day I play for little money," James reminisced despondently. "Other times they don't want me."

Off the pitch, he worked as a barber outside of Cape Town and fared a lot better. "Bro, you can be eating good down there," he declared fondly. "They have Mac-Doo-nalds, Steers, KFC and pizza!"

Brother James said he'd taken some English classes in South Africa, but he was mostly self-taught through movies and Rap music. Looking for a break, James came to Kilwa and hoped to find work at one of the high dollar mzungu hotels on the beach, but the market was tight. Sidelined, he began teaching English twice a week to the hotel staff and was barely getting by.

"Its hard, bro. Sometimes I'm not knowing money for food."

I had to admit, the guy really tried, and he was clever too. You see, Brother James was acutely aware of the budgetary constraints mzungu has when traveling across the Motherland. So, he had concocted a scheme to get leverage on the racket. Being that I'm all about cutting cost, I was game to hear about it.

Early one steamy morning, James and I made our way to the antiquities office. After a brief wait, a state official of incredible bulk arrived. You could tell by his physical disposition that nothing got by this guy. He was boss, proper. So, on his appearance, I flagged the operation, but James insisted it would work.

"Bro, we can do this," he protested.

Naively, I went along.

While the Big Man arranged the paper work, he asked specifically how I met James. I explained that I wanted to visit the island and by the grace of God, I'd come across a solid chap who volunteered his services. The Boss rocked his head back and glared at Brother James.

"Did you approach this man or did he contact you?" He growled tenaciously.

"We just met in town," James responded, slightly unnerved.

"So," the big man shouted at the top of his lungs. "You're at it again! You know the policy! You know how things are done!"

James protested vociferously, but his effort was promptly overruled by a clenched fist landing on a wooden desktop like a jack-boot to carton of eggs. Thump!

"Get out! Get out of this office!" The Boss shouted.

James scrambled away like a soiled rat, knocking ajar papers and pencils as he snatched his book bag off a desk. Afterwards, the Big Boss returned his attention to me. Here it comes, I thought. This guy is going to charge me with undercutting the program, cite a few other infractions for general purpose and then I'm gonna make my debut on "Locked up Abroad".

"Mr. Eric," he began in a very stern voice. "There are bad people here. Take care."

After giving his warning, Bosi Kubwa (that's Swahili for Big Boss) completed the paper work, I paid the fees and then he stamped the documents.

"There you are," he said in a friendlier tone and handed me the ticket. "Enjoy your visit, Mr. Eric. I know you will like the place."

Back out on the road, Brother James flew into a tirade of how people were ruining his life.

"Bro, those guides are making up stories about me," he yelled, still stinging from the exchange in the office. Apparently, his tactics had aggravated more than the Man. "They had me in jail for two days. I did nothing wrong and they make for me trouble."

It turned out that James had been detained on suspicion of undercutting the officially sanctioned prices and taking food off of other people's plates. After several days of reckoning, the hotel owner vouched for his legitimacy, but that experience only confirmed James anti-establishment view.

Regardless of the outcome, there was still a role for James to play, finding me a legitimate guide. You see, not only was I going to visit Kilwa, but I'd also planned on checking out the mysterious ruins on Sanje ya Kati (a small island further south).

Adamant about sticking to the official price sheet, the first guy was a real stiff.

"Kaka yangu," my brother, I began in Swahili. "This is Africa, we must bargain. There are no set prices here."

He grimaced painfully and then shook his head no, "hapana."

Brother James had been hovering about and indicated he knew another guide with a better understanding of business.

"Don't worry, G. I'll find him."

A little while later, a thin guy with a spotty goatee arrived at New Mjaka. He was dressed in market hand-me downs and a faded Yankees ball cap. Saidi Juma was friendly, good natured and ready to wheel and deal. Within ten minutes we set a plan to visit Kisiwani the next afternoon and tentatively organized an excursion to another island.

XX

The Shotgun Tour of Kilwa Kisiwani

Saidi and I made the passage on a small weather beaten dhow. Slow going, yet relaxing, the triangular sail whipped lazily against the mast as the vessel plied across gentle waves. A dark green crab scuttled in and out of the shadows as we headed towards the island.

Initially starting as a small trading station, Kilwa battled with other towns along the coast, snatching away the gold trade from Sofala, a settlement further to the south in Mozambique (the gold came from deep in the interior- which we'll explore later). As Kilwa grew wealthy, massive structures were built, coins minted and many buildings painted white. With a little thought, it's easy to imagine the early morning sun breaking across the ocean and illuminating the town with a radiant glow (in past times Kilwa was called the pearl of Zanj). The town was sacked by both the Portuguese and restless natives. It is written that most inhabitants were Bantu slaves ruled by a class of Arabs, Persians and Moors.

Thirty minutes later, the skipper moored against a stone jetty and Saidi sprung into action.

"Let us pass quickly," he commanded, and then pointed at the dark band of clouds drifting across the horizon. "It may rain soon."

Racing across the spongy ground, we trotted over the foundations of forgotten buildings and through swarms of ants (they were everywhere!). The slightest hesitation or pause in stride brought them charging up your legs and clamping into your flesh. After a mile or so, we reached the first set of ruins called Husuni Kubwa; a multi-tiered palace on a bluff overlooking a patch of mangroves. The white wash had flaked away long ago and the grayed coral held together by lime lay across the ground in fragmented chunks. The grounds still had a command position overlooking the water front. With a little imagination you can see the Portuguese fleet still anchored broadside just offshore.

Next door is Husuni Ndogo. Although heavily eroded, it still retains its rectangular shape and a medieval atmosphere. Its authority lay in the circular bastions staggered around the perimeter at regular intervals. The interior was a large courtyard that seemed like a place to find refuge in or secure large quantities of valuable goods. Kirkman, our archaeologist friend, refers to Kidogo as the most impressive and interesting building that has been uncovered in East Africa.

"I believe this to be where the gold was kept," Saidi said, as I paced the interior and sized up the dimensions.

Next, we trekked towards the island's interior, passing deep wells and small conglomerations of mud and stick huts. Along the way, Saidi greeted everyone we met on a first name basis. At a massive baobab tree he halted the advance.

"These are the tombs of the Kilwa Sultans," Saidi announced, and then pointed at a small conglomeration of stout constructions.

"Just the Sultans?" I asked to appear interested, but the tombs were drab and my attention drifted further ahead.

"The families are here too," he replied. "If you look close, the protrusions and rounded edges show if it's a man or woman buried here."

So far I felt disconnected from the place. I didnt know if it was the head cold or Saidi's pace, but I just wasn't locking on the way I normally did at other historic sites.

Noticing that my interest in the tombs had waned, Saidi smiled and signaled to move on.

Treking along some muddy flats, we rounded our way into Makutani, a complex of tall buildings and massive city walls enclosing five acres of open pitch. Freshly tuck pointed, the whole complex had been renovated and the grounds maintained. This place had a certain vibrancy and you could sense the throngs of people who lived here centuries before.

"This is the palace," Saidi said and then pointed up. The remains of multi storied buildings towered overhead as we crept through tight courtyards and narrow passage ways. It was solid, reinforced on the outside with buttresses. The hallowed remains yearned for exploration like haunting voices waiting to be heard, but Saidi kept pushing us forward. So, I glanced at the waterfront just long enough to catch a fleeting image of seaborne raiders charging across the pitch, hear the muffled clank of a saber and feel the dry "pop" of a discharging musket.

Circling back around towards the jetty we came upon two mosques. First, was the Great Mosque. Because of its eighteen cupolas and barrel vaults, Kirkman (our archaeologist buddy) refers to it as the finest mosque from medieval Africa. Further along, there was a smaller domed mosque, partially collapsed, but in a way that gave it an air of intrigue.

The tour concluded along the water's edge at Gereza, an old Omani Fort, Kisiwani's most prominent feature. Initially, the fort was built by the Portuguese. Later, Arabs made extensive modifications giving it a stout appearance. Landward, it seemed impenetrable, but the fort hasn't fared so well on the seaward side. Being right on the water, large sections have been washed away, exposing the original work of the Portuguese.

Despite a rapid assault, it had taken three hours to complete the mission. Due to the cost of it all, I came away empty, like something of value had been snatched from my hand never to be seen again. This was because of the pricing. A smarter plan would be to sell a ticket for multiple day access to the island (just like in Ethiopia), catch transport at the local price and then have the option to hire a guide rather than being led around. As indicated in the preceding paragraphs, such interference can dampen my psychic abilities to see back into time. Regardless, Kilwa was merely a side show. The real reason I'd come down the coast was to visit Sanje ya Kati.

XXI

Mystery Ruins of Sanje ya Kati

Back in the 1950's reports began to filter up into the industrialized world about a unique set of ruins on a small island called Sanje ya Kati. There, a British archaeologist named Gervase Matthews discovered oblong structures and a citadel with sixteen foot walls. The island is well off the main track. Reaching it required a boat and a guide. So, I brought Saidi Juma back into the plan for twenty-five bucks. Another forty-five secured a day's outing on the Sea Taxi, a narrow wooden launch with a blue canopy and a white hull streaked with rust marks.

At 7:30 am we boarded up and the pilot angled south into the channel separating the islands with the mainland. It took just over one hour to span the choppy waters between Kilwa Masoka and Sanje ya Kati. There'd been rain on the way over, but the clouds thinned out as we rounded the island's western side and made for the sandy shores of its southern tip. A handful of dhows and dugouts were spread across the beach and a small gathering, alerted by the incessant drone of the Sea Taxi's outboard motor, watched our arrival (the island is also home to an obscure fishing community).

With the launch just off shore, Saidi and I waded through knee deep water; sinking to our ankles in the muddy bottoms as we slogged toward dry land while the pilot stayed onboard.

"We have to organize with the village chairman," Saidi smiled, while lacing up his shoes. "After that, everything should be okay."

Snatching one of the idlers, Saidi led the three of us around a patch of mangroves and headed for a collection of huts.

"This is the place," he said, and then went to the door of a rudimentary dwelling.

A shirtless man in his early fifties emerged from the shadowy interior. Although his goatee was speckled with gray, he was still fit, undoubtedly from the physical demands of living in an undeveloped environment.

"Mzee, kuonyesha hii mzungu ngome ya zamani," Saidi said to the old man, indicating that I wanted to see something.

"Ehhhhh," Mzee's eyes lit up while he stretched like a man wrenched from a late morning slumber. After adjusting his hat, he retrieved a machete from a little shack and then pointed towards a tangle of green vegetation.

"Eric, it's just there," Saidi indicated.

Following a lightly worn path into the brush we came upon the vague outline of a linear structure shielded by a patch of thorny trees and stringy vines.

"Have him clear away that undergrowth," I said, eager to see what would be revealed.

While the old man went to work, Saidi and I followed the path a bit further and found another partially exposed structure.

"I believe this to be a mosque," he stated, and then pointed to the squat remains of what may have been something much larger in the past.

Looking closely, the squared masonry had been tuck-pointed and the uneven joints flattened out with concrete or mortar, indicating the structure had undergone some degree of restoration. It was plausible this building could have been converted into a mosque, but who's to say originally it wasn't a treasury or an armory?

Returning to the first spot, the chairman had exposed five rows of square blocks. More layers were below the surface of the ground. Its overall plan was a long rectangle, fitting Matthews' description of an oblong structure or building. Entering the compartment I crouched down and ran my fingers over the stone work, eyeing the masonry left to right. Coursed masonry is what makes this site so distinctive from the other ruins along the Swahili Coast. It's a building technique where blocks of stone are squared and then stacked in an orderly manner rather than chunks of coral fitted together and skimmed over with cement like material.

From Pate Island, to Jumba la Mtwana and all sites along the Tanzania's coast and the Zanzibar archipelago the building style and material is nearly always the same; stacked chunks of coral, but here, the builders used coursed masonry; blocks of stone stacked in an orderly manner. After making this comparison, the questions begs, who built these ruins?

If we turn to page 177 of Basil Davidson's "The Lost cities of Africa", he writes "it's in the earliest of the coast trading settlement so far traced; and its iron using culture may well have been pre-Islamic by several centuries". Davidson goes on to add that the builders may have come from southern Arabia or southern India. Considering the trade routes of the Indian Ocean and their age, it is very plausible. Possibly, it could have been the greatest traders of the ancient world, the Phoenicians.

In brief, they were tribesman from the Sinai Peninsula who'd taken to the waves. Using Biremes, single mast galleys with two levels of oars (the ship of the ancient world) they plied the waters of the Mediterranean and built trading centers all the way to Spain. Their travels took them to West Africa, the Azores and into the setting sun (in the 1960s the remains of a Phoenician ship were discovered off the coast of Brazil). Possibly, their greatest journey was circumnavigating the African continent over a thousand years ago. When considering the technology of the time, it seems a daunting feat, almost impossible, but in recent times the voyage has been repeated, twice. In 1989, a recreation of Egyptian sailing vessel named the Pount was piloted around Africa in two and half years. As recent as 2008 a galley replica called the Phoenicia (constructed from the specifications determined by various artifacts) completed the expedition as well.

At one time, there appears to have been some solid evidence of this feat. In his book "Unsolved Mysteries of Southern Africa" Rob Marsh writes about a strange wreck discovered in South Africa. In the 1880s, scores of planking were dug up along with a 60-70 foot mast. Even a hundred years later in the 1980s, the South African government conducted an extensive investigation, including carbon dating wood artifacts collected from the site. The result, something built from timber that originated in the northern hemisphere 500-1900 years ago.

"Are there any more ruins on the island," I asked Saidi, while pondering over the builders of these mysterious ruins.

Saidi conversed with the chairman; shaking his head sideways, the old man answered in a low tone.

"Everything is here," Saidi relayed.

"This is it?" I replied, feeling like I was on the cusp of an important discovery, yet coming up a bit empty handed.

"Hapana. There is more."

"Where?"

"Just here."

Saidi signaled to Mzee to keep chopping. So, he had at it, cutting into the bush perpendicular from the trail. Chips of white pulpy wood sliced through the air each time the machete blade struck a tree or branch; Saidi and I followed in anticipation. After a few minutes of exertion, the chairman opened a hole through the leafy vegetation, reaching a larger wall shielded by clumps of grasses and weeds.

"Saidi!" I shouted. "Have Mzee hack everything away from the stone work. We need to find out what's back there!"

Saidi made a swinging motion with his forearm and the chairman cleared the rest of the undergrowth, hacking away low hanging branches until the remains of several compartments were exposed.

"It's the foundation for a large building," I said. "Each one of these sections has an entry point".

"Yes, it was very big at one time," Saidi seconded, as he followed me into the ruins.

In the largest area, I retrieved a tape measure from my bag of sensitive items and made a spot measurement with Saidi's assistance. From the top to the floor the wall's height stood almost four feet. While recording the measurements in my journal, the chairman mumbled to Saidi.

"Come, Eric. There is more," Saidi translated.

Dark clouds converged overhead again and unleashed a steady rain (the incessant patter of droplets playing out across the leafy vegetation). Cinching down his ball cap the chairman continued his travail, slashing with such tenacity that a shroud of steam lifted away from his back. Deeper in the brush the ground took a slightly higher grade. Underfoot, traces of long forgotten structures poked through the dead vegetation. Stopping momentarily, the chairman wiped the sweat from his brow. After a few more heavy swings, he tugged away a mesh of leafy vines, exposing large coursed blocks stacked together in a cone like form. Firmly rooted within the joints and spanning across the layers of stone, trees had taken root, giving the stout construction a lost appearance.

"This is a watch tower," Saidi indicated. The chairman grunted in agreement.

Behind the small bastion, more walls poked out of the mud and up through the soggy piles of dead leaves. The ruins looked substantial and clearing it out would have been a major under taking. So, I settled for a casual observation, but before I could take it all in, the chairman indicated there was another section to see.

Continuing onward, we came to another wall pitching slightly to one side. With Saidi's assistance, I made another spot measurement; fifty-two inches high. That's just over four feet, nearly three quarters shy of the 16 foot tall Citadel described by archaeologist Mathew, but the discrepancy is easily explained.

"You see, this site is unprotected. So, when local people need the stone to build, they can just take," Saidi said, and then motioned his hands as if heavy lifting were being done. Just like in Ethiopia, the ruins along Swahili-land were often treated as a resource base by the locals.

Angling wide through the brush, we slogged across muddy fields strewn with shards of broken pottery, back into the tangle of foliage and then out the other side and landed back at the chairman's hut. Hurriedly, the chairman climbed up a palm tree and liberated a clump of coconuts. They landed on the compressed sand with a hollow thump. Using a smaller knife, he carved away the outer husk and then whittled away a circular piece on the top of the coconut. We drank heartily.

While enjoying the velvety swill of the island's house beverage, I pondered what the yield would be after sweeping the site with a high end metal detector. Surely there had to be a cache of old coins somewhere on the island. Saidi indicated there'd been a handful of digs, one as recent as 2004, but only one piece of gold had been unearthed. "Very small" he'd reiterated, but then immediately retracted the statement.

That's interesting I thought. Having only been skimmed over, maybe pieces of gold turned up from time-to-time, pieces of a much larger cache that the villages have been seeking out through the years.

XXII

The Next Island Over

After downing a couple tubs of Mother Nature's finest, we loaded back on the launch and then plowed across a small straight to another island. Diligently, the skipper piloted into a small cove, around a collection of dhows, into a patch of mangroves and then stopped just short of the shore. Saidi and I made land fall after splashing through ankle deep water.

Outside a hut, a group of fishermen hovered over a boiling pot of stew. Freshly removed from the fire, a stout pile of ugali (a loaf of cornmeal, rough in texture and bland in taste) steamed away off to the side. Saidi greeted the men, pinched a handful of ugali and plucked a piece of fish from the pot. A grizzly looking chap angled my way and spoke in a deep drawn out voice, "You are welcome."

"Asante." I replied, and then waved off the invitation with two open hands.

Back on the trail, we traced over another ubiquitous sandy path that parted tall grassy areas and occasionally intersecting other paths. Some traveled frequently, others slowly being reclaimed by the island. Patches of dark clouds tumbled overhead and the rains grew steadier, but there was no relief. It was still a steam bath, the humidity draping around my body and squeezing it like a sponge.

When a gap opened between us Saidi stopped and looked back disparagingly. "What is wrong with you?"

"Man, I'm tired,"

"What?" He asked with a puzzled look. "I thought you lived for this stuff."

When we were setting up the gig, I'd run my mouth a bit about being an adventurer and having been published a couple of times. But after the adrenaline rush of Sanje, I was fighting with that head cold again, and the prospect of seeing another Swahili city seemed a bit repetitive.

"Dude, why you gotta call me out for?" I responded defensively.

Saidi snickered and then lit back on the trail, but it seemed like we were just retracing our steps.

"My friend," I asked. "Where are you taking us?"

"I've only been to this site a couple of times," he replied, meaning he didn't remember the exact location.

When we came upon another hut Saidi asked the matriarch in residence for directions, but she just shook her head. So, we trudged further along until finding an old man sheltered under a patch of trees. Saidi conversed with him a bit and then turned around and smiled.

"He knows the place."

Taking a new direction, we charged across water logged flats, through fields of wet grass and then stopped at another patch of woods. Dark green leaves glistened under the sheen of rain water; the downpour had increased. At first I didn't notice anything, but closer examination revealed something behind the glistening foliage. Monolithic in appearance, the last standing walls of a lost city were shrouded by bushes and heavy branches. It was the standard style of construction; large chunks of coral plastered together. Inside the canopy the fragmented remains of broken masonry were piled up and covered by layers of leaves, slowly being absorbed back into the elements.

"What is this place called?" I asked.

Saidi spoke rapidly to the old man. Mzee replied just as fast.

"This is Sanje Mjoma," Saidi commented, "but the government is not taking care of the place."

Pulling off to the side, Saidi motioned we should toss the guy a few Shillings.

"You're joking, right?" I asked him sternly. "I mean the guy showed up to the party and didn't even bring a machete. Now he wants a cut?"

Saidi chuckled lightly, "Don't worry. I'll take care of him."

There was one more ruin to see. It was on the north end of the island. To reach the site, the pilot skillfully inserted us into a rocky cove. Hastily, we scaled up a coral embankment and tracked our way along a path. Minutes later we arrived at another site.

At the time of my visit, Songo Mnara was undergoing a massive renovation. Many of the buildings had been cleaned up and were easily accessed. The structures were large and spread out. Prowling through the empty shells I could only wonder what phantoms and ghosts swirled about the place under a full moon.

The way out was through a watery tunnel in the mangroves. Pushing forward, the stagnant water inched up our legs and past our knees. By the time we cleared the mangroves it was mid-thigh.

"Soon it will get deep," Saidi warned.

"How deep is deep?" I asked with a bit of consternation.

"Maybe three to four meters."

"What about the crocodiles?" I asked, just as the water lapped at my waist.

"There are no crocodiles," he replied sharply.

As the water inched up to my chest, I held my bag of sensitive items overhead and began a one-armed dog paddle. The launch was only a few meters away, but I felt a little jumpy.

"What about the sharks?"

Saidi didn't respond.

"I hate sharks, Saidi. I hate 'em."

"Then make for the boat quickly, my friend!"

Back in the safety of New Mjaka, I fell in for the night, totally knackered by the day's outing. Saidi stopped by and asked if I was up for a few rounds of fire water. It would have been a great way to finish the visit but, regretfully, I had to decline. Thirty minutes later, Brother James arrived and got straight to the point.

"Brother Eric, I told you my situation," he began. "There is no food and rent is unpaid for two months."

Man, I felt for the guy, but there wasn't much I could do, especially since I was managing my cash as tight as possible. He'd already worked a few sodas out of me and the previous day I sprung for breakfast. Heck, I'd only been eating one meal a day myself and that was fried eggs and chipsi (French fries). I simply didn't have it, and besides, if I passed out dough every time someone asked for it, what would be left for me?

"Pal, let me tell you how it is," I began, in a slow drawn out manner. "These days it's tough all over, get it?"

James idled for a few minutes, grumbled something unintelligible and then faded away into the night.

XXIII

Intercession

After a night back in the Dar City Palace, I grabbed a bus to Ubungo Bus Terminal for a ticket to Zimbabwe. The boulevard out was a half-finished public works project that seemed a decade behind schedule. What should have been a major four lane artery was reduced to two lanes; outbound still on the road and the inbound grinding its way through the muddy soup along the shoulder. Cars, trucks, and buses edged out the pedestrians; the side view mirrors on the largest vehicles coming in at eye level. Watch out! The last thing you want is to be knocked down and skinned up along the roadside. Surely, the flesh eating virus, or worse, was lurking around in the muck.

Within seconds of jumping out at a busy intersection, I was accosted by a vagrant.

"Where do you go?" He shouted over the rumble of slow moving vehicles.

"Nowhere, get it?"

"Do you want Arusha?" he persisted.

"I want you to get out of my face, Jack! Understand?" I replied, but he ignored the message. So, I pulled a Crazy Ivan twice, pivoting left and weaving through the mob, but the shake didn't work. He hung on like a shadow, matching my every move and rambling on about how I was making life difficult for him.

"Why do you make trouble in my country?" He shouted.

Fighting back the urge to deck him, I headed towards a couple of guys posted up by a gate.

"Kuna polisi hapa?" I asked in Swahili.

"You want the police, what for?" The skinny one responded.

"I want to buy a ticket, but this knuckle-beak won't get off my back."

"Where are you going?"

"Harare."

"Okay, let's go this side," he said and then pointed to Room 22 along row of ticket offices.

When the idiot started up about "my country" and "my job" again, skinny man's side kick, a portly fellow with a double chin, gave him an opened handed thump to the middle of the chest. This time he got the message.

The Harare booking office was in a long row of single story, single room concrete offices. Company names and destinations were painted on the outside and pictures of big buses were taped up on the interior walls. A handful of idlers looked on earnestly.

"Can you please show me your passport?" The ticket man asked.

"In front of everyone? Let's move operations behind this partition." I suggested, concerned about any unwanted attention.

Back in the office, I handed him eighty bucks and he gave me a ticket to Zimbabwe.

At 5:30 the next morning, I climbed onboard a massive red beast. Dimly lit and quickly filling with passengers, it was only short the birds to fully qualify as a chicken bus. The overhead storage bins were already packed to the hilt and cardboard boxes were wedged underneath every single seat. After loosening up some space overhead, I stashed my duffle bag and secured it with my cable lock. My bag of sensitive items would rest on my lap for the duration. Several minutes later, a sleepy-eyed woman sunk into the seat on my right. I greeted her in Swahili and she nodded cordially, though her eyes seemed apprehensive.

There was no ventilation or air conditioning on the bus. Luckily, I had scored a window seat and adjusted the window in accordance to the speed of the vehicle. By mid-morning I had settled into the ride, my mind freed up from the filth and clutter of Dar until I heard a muffled gag emanate from the meaty lass on my right. She had a hanky clamped over her mouth and a worried look in her eyes.

"Turn your head! Turn you head!" I shouted, hoping she'd angle to the aisle before it was too late.

I'd just gotten over my fears of cholera when a stream of warm watery vomit speckled with bright yellow chunks splashed across my leg, soaked though my linen trousers and then washed up on my skin. Aw cripes, I grimaced, and then the fear of contracting a tropical disease raced though my head, again!

Around noon, a DVD player fired up and Tanzanian movies subtitled in English played out on a TV mounted overhead. Outside, the bus whipped past thin herds of zebra and giraffe, around rolling hills, through rains big and small and by a jack-knifed truck. Late in the afternoon two hurried looking men dressed in civilian attire boarded the bus.

"Passports! Passports!" They demanded. After comparing everyone's face with their identity papers they quickly departed.

Starting back up, we speed into the night arriving at the border around 10:30 pm. It had taken just over sixteen hours to cross Tanzania lengthwise. When considering you can fly between Chicago and London twice within that time span, it seems like a long time. But fathom this! A similar journey made by Burton and Speke (two Victorian explorers) during the 1850's would have taken months.

At first opportunity, I got out and walked around the town, Tunduma. With exception to some small stands illuminated by candles, nearly all the dukas had closed for the night. In preparation for the journey, I had stocked up on ginger snap biscuits, water, and two bottles of warm Coca-Cola. By no means was I going to eat any food on this trip. There were no facilities on the bus and snacking at a road side dive would surely be disagreeable with my bowels. Fasting was the only way to go.

Cold and cramped, I spent the night on the bus dozing off from time-to-time and shifting in my seat with great regularity. Just before dawn, the shop lights came on one-by-one and then music started playing everywhere. Barefoot and dressed in soiled clothes, a gang of laborers rinsed down the exterior of the bus with dirty water while the bus crew lit sticks of incense inside. Slowly, small groups of people began to trickle across the border. I fell in behind some fellow passengers.

On the other side, the Zambian immigrations officials were a terrible lot. They'd just finished shredding a couple of Ugandans when I handed an officer my passport. His eyes flickered menacingly as he turned each page, occasionally sizing me up and then returning his attention to the small blue book in his hand.

"What do you want in Zambia?" he snapped in an uncompromising tone.

"Just a transit visa," I replied. "I'm heading to Zimbabwe."

"You have seven days in my country," he shouted and then stamped my passport.

Half the day was wasted parked on the Zambian side. At 2 in the afternoon we raced off again across the backend of Zambia until landing at Lusaka bus terminal. It was 1 in the morning. The piles of debris found in such places had been swept away, but there were a hoard of people rolled up in blankets and sleeping on the concrete. The shops were plenty and big green insects fluttered through the air. A handful of men chased them down and corralled the catch in 1-litre plastic bottles.

"They are so nice fried," a taxi driver assured me while holding up his take for the evening. Dozens of the leggy bugs squirmed atop each other in the narrow confines of the container.

Another gang of labors showed up, this time running a relay on the dozens of cardboard boxes stashed under the seats and in the back of the bus. Within minutes, a massive pile formed up in the parking lot, only to be broken down and carted off into the night.

At 3 am, the beast fired back up and the driver attacked the road with an unrelenting fervor. It was pitch black out. The only sense of direction was forward on a downward grade. The bus tilted precariously as we rounded the turns and the dips got steeper and steeper like we were plunging down from a plateau.

Several hours later, we exited Zambia and entered Zimbabwe just as the sun began to rise. Our passports promptly stamped by tall men in crisp uniforms who conversed in firm, but professional tones. There was a delay while Customs shook down the small time traders. Just after noon, we landed in Harare on a refreshingly sunny day with big blue skies and puffy white clouds drifting over head.

Although it had taken two and a half days to complete the journey, I'd made it! I hadn't eaten anything except biscuits and crisps (potato chips) the whole time. I'd nursed a two liter of water and the warm cokes Id kept for emergencies lasted for about a day. My trousers were still scarred by the stain of vomit and I was dead tired. So, the first order of business was to arrange accommodations.

As you've seen, I'm always out to lowball costs, but in Harare twenty-five bucks got you jack squat! So, I dumped forty-five bones at a freshly painted place that looked like the motor lodges my old man used to stop at when I was a kid. As you can guess, getting cleaned up was second order of business. For the last day and a half, I'd been dreaming of a hot shower, but was I in for a surprise: there was no running water at all!

"It's Saturday," the front desk clerk announced. "They are doing maintenance, but it can come back anytime."

You are correct, sir. The water came back on at about five the next morning, icy cold!

Zimbabwe: the Kingdom of Stone

XXIV

The Road to Bulawayo

Thirty bucks got a seat on a big red double-decker called Pathfinder Bus Services. The price was a bit high, but after suffering on the beast for almost three days, who cared? It had big reclining seats. So I rocked back and fully extended my legs. There was also air conditioning and an onboard toilet that could be used for "short calls". The entertainment system was fully functional and showed black American TV shows and movies. The rig even came with young ladies dressed up like flight attendants. They distributed cool beverages and snack packs at regular intervals.

Outside Harare the road was in good order and we spun evenly along the N4, the two lane highway linking Harare to Bulawayo. Sporadically, the older woman sitting next to me made conversation about the similarities in climate between Zimbabwe and America. The weather was nice here, that's for sure. Puffy white clouds drifted across big blue skies and the air was always like a fresh spring day.

Sitting high up with a clear view of the roadside was nice for a change. So, after finishing the last few pages of the "Jewels of Opar" (an Edgar Rice Burroughs novel I'd nabbed at a second hand shop in Mombasa), I watched the bush flash by and thought of the stone cities scattered across Zimbabwe.

Some people think that Great Zimbabwe is the only ruins in southern Africa, but it's not. The breadth of "Zimbabwe Style" sites found in southern Africa is far and wide. Aerial surveys have detected thousands of ancient sites dotting the landscape. The ruins are diverse, anything from small seemingly insignificant walls to massive structures decorated with ornamental patterns. Zimbabwe has the highest concentration of these ruins, but adventurers can see the Tati ruins in Botswanna, the Machema ruins in South Africa and the mountain kingdoms of Niamara and Magure, both in Mozambique. On many occasions elliptical enclosures and/or walls are incorporated with natural rock formations.

These ruins were brought to mainstream attention by Great White Hunters like Frederick Selous and Henry Hartley who'd ventured into the remote and unknown bush searching for game. Along with a wide array of wildlife trophies, they came upon strange stone structures, often overgrown with dense bush and shrouded by trees hundreds of years old. Surprisingly, these hardened adventurers were not the first Europeans to witness such ruins. Decades, and perhaps a century before, Portuguese missionaries accompanied by soldiers penetrated the interior and spread the Lord's word. Some of their artifacts have turned up in a handful of the ruins.

As prospectors and adventurers followed, gold fields pocketed with ancient mines (seemingly dug and worked by people small in stature) became known. Gold is very dense yet easily shaped and physically manipulated. It forms when hot fluids rise towards the earth's surface and cool off. The liquefied gold elements solidify in the cracks and splits of solid rock to form veins. Through time, the rock erodes away and the exposed gold breaks up into smaller pieces and settles in and around rivers and creeks. This is known as placer gold.

It was also discovered that the ruins held a bounty too; gold smelting furnaces, gold dust, gold beads and other ornaments-some weighing 6 oz. each. Crucibles (a pot used to melt metal) were found still holding gold. When word got out that these riches were literally laying about and easily picked from the ruins the hunt was on! Two of the most successful treasure seekers were W.G. Neal and G. Johnson. They operated a company called Rhodesian Ancient Ruins, LTD. The men worked hard covering many sites and found much gold. At a complex called Dhlo-Dhlo the team recovered 700 oz of gold bead and wires (this is on top of an earlier haul of 641 oz, collected by Frederick Russell Burnham, aka the King of the Scouts).

Many people will argue that the work of the Rhodesian Ancient Ruins caused damage to the physical integrity of the sites. This is true. However, their endeavors also generated a significant amount of documentation regarding the condition and style of these ruins. Work, that if Neal and Johnson did not engage in treasure hunting, may have never occurred with such detail or while the stone structures were still in existence. The recipient of this trove of documentation was Richard Nicklin Hall. He used it in his book "The Ancient Ruins of Rhodesia".

Anyone interested in the study of lost cities in Africa should add this book to the stack. Despite being over one hundred years old, it's packed with a wealth of information, like detailed descriptions of several hundred sites, old photographs showing the state of the ruins at the turn of the 19th century and a collection of diagrams depicting the layouts of selected ruins. There are also chapters dedicated to history, exploration and gold mining. The book also comes with a huge fold out map of southern Africa (centered on Rhodesia). The names of towns and physical features are printed in black ink and the names of ruins are slightly bolder in red ink.

Granite blocks have been used to build the structures, but on occasion diorite, white quartz, ribbon slate and iron stone have been worked into the stone buildings. When it comes to examining the building techniques, not all of the ruins are equal. Hall defines the styles of construction in four different periods. They are: the first period, characterized by massive solidarity and symmetry, rounded walls and built on an elliptical plan. There is a superior quality of workmanship and they are set in rock foundations. Squared entrances, right angles and check patterns abound in the second period. Larger blocks of stone set in a circular form demonstrate the third period and finally, the fourth period is characterized by small circular stone buildings made from crudely stacked blocks pillaged from other sites.

Decorative masonry observed at the ruins comes in five patterns: dentelle, chevron, herring-bone, sloping block and check. Rows of squared stone situated flat so that a corner edge points out from the face of the wall is the dentelle style. A row of stone set lengthwise at alternating 45 degree angles is the chevron style. Two rows of stone (a top and bottom row) set lengthwise so they meet at a 45 degree angle and point to the right symbolizes herring-bone. Half a row of herring-bone is the sloping block. Stones set so that a gap alternates between them (like a game board) is the check pattern.

Great Zimbabwe, Dhlo-Dhlo and Khami are the largest ruins (we will visit two of these). After leafing through the pages of Hall's publication, I found several other interesting sites with storied histories. For starters, the number three ruin of the four citadels known as the Mundi Ruins should be called the slaughterhouse. It's 160 feet in diameter and has walls 14 feet high. Here, adventurers uncovered a grave with 72 ounces of gold and also found 230 ounces of gold "cake" (bars perhaps). There were also charred human remains and an abundance of twisted gold ornament scattered about, like they'd been torn from human limbs.

Set in an elliptical shape, the Chum Ruins cover a half an acre. At five feet high the walls are on the shorter side, but there are nine foot buttresses built into the exterior. The interior is subdivided into large and small compartments. The skeletal remains of a seven foot tall man, his shin bones nearly two feet in length, were found with "immense gold bangles". Sixteen ounces of gold accompanied the remains.

The Thabas Imamba Ruins are a massive circular formation 200 feet in diameter and set upon a cliff. It has endured multiple occupations and suffered accordingly. The smallest compartments of the ruins have been filled with stone blocks taken from the highest portions of the original walls. Some stones have been restacked so many times that there are examples of 2nd, 3rd and the 4th period masonry within the structure. However, the most intriguing detail about the place is that a king of the Momba people was skinned alive by Amaswazie savages.

Umnukwana ruins are characterized by a massive wall 200 hundred feet long, 13 feet thick and 17 feet high. A large boulder is part of the exterior wall. The interior consists of a number of small compartments worked in with and around six large boulders. The remains of seven people were found strewn about the ruins.

Two more sites that stand out from the total are the Check Ruins, distinguished by a stone pattern that covers the entire surface of the outer and inner walls, and the Clay Zimbabwe. This site, consisting of two circles twenty-five feet in diameter and seventeen high, are formed entirely of clay (though more recently than the stone ruins).

In closing, it should be noted that a considerable amount of desecration occurred while on the hunt for gold, but to claim European adventurers are the only culprit is just untrue. As we know from the journey so far, lost cities and ruins function as a resource for building materials for local people. Specifically to the Zimbabwes, it has been noted that African tribes who reoccupied the ruins had the tendency to knock down the upper walls and fill in the inner spaces. Also, baboons have been observed flipping rocks in search of small snacks and the region is prone to tectonic activities.

Six hours later, the bus stopped in the heart of Bulawayo. The city proper was laid out on a grid plan. The streets are long, broad and accept slanted parking. Most of the cars were boxy, like they'd been manufactured in the 80's and the 90's. Traffic congestion was almost nonexistent, a far cry from the bumper-to-bumper grind of Mombasa and Dar es Salam. The tallest buildings in the central business district had big signs on the front like Meikles, H&S, and Geekays.

Bulawayo is Zimbabwe's second largest city. It has its roots with the Ndebele people. The name comes from the Ndebele word Kobuluwayo, meaning "place where he is being killed".

After a series of skirmishes known as the Matabele Wars, European adventurers gained the upper hand and forged the foundations for what would be the modern city. In its infancy, Bulawayo had the reputation of being a rough town, but would go on to host a wide range of industry and manufacturing as well as the terminus for the national rail system.

Most people in town are of dark brown complexion. There are a few Indians and a handful of whites in the crowd. Women had a liking for big floppy hats. Every once in awhile someone called me "papa" or "sir" and the taxi driver who got me out to my accommodations even gave me a "yes boss".

Tucked away off of 12th street in "the suburbs" was a one story house called Packers Paradise Lodge. I'd read about in my travel guide. You get in through a massive green gate that rolls open to the side. The grounds were watered daily; the grass was green and the plants broad and leafy. In back, there was a lorry park with two safari vehicles parked in the shade and an out building called the dorm. The lobby had a couch and TV and the reception desk was sheltered by a thatched roof awning. A Zimbabwe mama and her daughter managed the place, but it was owned by someone else.

Inside the main building there were a handful of rooms with shared facilities. They went for fifty bucks a pop, a bit high.

"I'm really looking for something around twenty a night," I told the girl.

"Come to the back," she instructed, "I want you to see the dorm".

The out building was a bit confined and someone had already settled in. I was about to move on when she indicated there was one more spot and then dashed off for the key.

"This is the last one," she said, when she returned and then guided me into a gated patio and through a back door. Inside was a long narrow room. Half was a kitchen with running water and the rest was a bedroom with two slim bunks on each side. The place was spotless.

"It's slow now. So, just have this for yourself," she offered.

"For twenty a night?" I confirmed.

"Why not?"

Talk about a score. I still had to share the facilities with other guests, but so what. There wasn't the wretched stank of stale piss.

Nor was there a decade worth of dust and grit layered up on every flat surface. The linens were crisp and white and for the first time I slept with the lights out, never once worrying about insects (or worse).

Five bucks got a massive breakfast of eggs, toast, sausage, bacon and coffee served up at a four person dinette the next morning. At the table, there was a young couple from Switzerland who had traveled in from Mozambique and was headed north. On previous trips they'd journeyed to Mexico and Brazil. Opposite me was Ian, a geologist from South Africa who bought tailings (byproducts left over from old mining operations) from an old copper mine and then shipped the containers to Johannesburg for further refinement.

"There's still forty percent copper in that slag," he boasted.

After eating, I made my way into town passing a three foot monitor lizard prowling along the roadside. Khami was about twelve miles outside of town. There wasn't a clear shot on public transport and Packers wanted eighty bucks for a ride. I needed a way out there, three hours at the site and then a ride back into town at a much friendlier price. So, I went to the streets and worked over the taxi drivers for something nicer. After a couple of close calls, a guy named Peter ran the calculations, deliberated for a minute and then gave me a quote. "Forty dollars. Yes, that is fair."

"Deal," I said, and then stuck my hand out for a firm handshake. "Pick me up at 10 am tomorrow morning."

Even though I'd already shook on it, I swung by the Tourist Information Center to verify the price.

"Only forty," the attendant repeated and his dark eye brows arched high up into a wrinkled forehead, "and he'll wait three hours? That is a very good price!"

Back at Packers, Ian, the geologist, was pacing the garden. Before I headed into town, he said he wanted to talk about something. So, I guess he'd been waiting for me to get back.

At 55, Ian had thinning sandy-gray hair and weathered blue eyes. He wore tattered clothing and limped around on deteriorating sandals. A small back pack with all his gear hung from his shoulder, because he was "traveling lightly".

"You still interested in treasure?" Ian asked in a hushed tone.

During breakfast the conversation had shifted into prospecting, gold mining and then eventually to lost gold. "Yeah, like what."

"Last year, a big meteorite was found near Gurve village," he said. "A company of soldiers hauled it off in a 2.5 ton truck."

Now I know what you're thinking, this isn't exactly gold, but there's a lot of dough to be had in space rocks. The trade in meteorites is big business. The recovery of meteorites can be high risk. Adventurers span the globe for this kind of treasure and like any other fortune seekers, can get robbed, jailed or cheated. Because of the lack of foliage the arctic and the desert regions produce the greatest yields. However, fine specimens have been recovered from wooded areas and from the bottom of lakes. Once in safe hands, these specimens can be sold as a whole, or, depending on the type, cut into plate-sized pieces.

Ian claimed to have already recovered one meteorite, but foolishly declared it when dragging it back into South Africa. "Man, I got hit with 80% taxes," he grimaced painfully. "But I still made some money."

"So, what's the deal?"

"Right now it's holed up at Gweru barracks under the protection of a high ranking officer. We have to get it out of there," he indicated, as if it were the leader of the opposition and being detained by the establishment. "That thing is worth money."

"How much?" I asked.

"The going rate is somewhere between $10 $100 a gram and it weighs at least 1000kg," Ian said under his breath, like he'd already given out too many details.

"Okay, how about this. We'll get some machine guns, hire a driver and set it free the old fashioned way," I said, jokingly.

"That could have been done twenty years ago, but not now," he replied, and shook his head. "We need money."

"How much money?"

Ian's back of the envelop calculations came to $50,000, minimum.

"And we need to meet the right guy, or we could get swindled," he added.

Fifty thousand was way out of my league. So, gradually, I extracted myself from the conversation, but before I could, Ian hit me up for forty dollar loan.

"I'll have it back to you by tomorrow, promise."

"Ah, things are a little tight right now," I replied. "In fact, my people need to wire me some dough. I'm short too."

XXV

The Kingdom of Stone

When Peter arrived the following morning, there was already a fare in the front seat. She was in her early twenties and very interested in my take on Bulawayo.

"Seems like a nice place," I replied, because of the weather and the laid back pace on the streets.

"Just say it's slow," she giggled, like I was being overly polite. "But if you want to see a commotion, have a girl walk in town with a mini-skirt on."

Peter glanced over and smirked lightly.

"What will happen?" I asked, anticipating a story about street side shenanigans.

"Men can just tear her clothes off," she said, and then laughed mockingly.

"Are you sure?"

"Yes!" She proclaimed loudly. "I saw it myself. A girl just came through the bus station in a skirt short-short. The men said, if you want to go naked we can help you, and then they removed all her clothing."

"Driver!" I said to Peter. "Do acts of barbarism still occur in the modern era?"

"They can," Peter acknowledged, and then broke into a mild chuckle.

The girl alighted at a big department store and Peter drove us out of town, passing the six massive cooling towers of the local power plant. It appeared functional, but the broken windows and eroded concrete made it out like a relic of a lost industrial age. After passing through several police check points (on the edge of town) we rolled unhindered through the countryside on a well maintained road; country music played as we drove along.

To some, the Khami ruins are considered to be the second best ruins in Zimbabwe. The site consists of eleven different structures. You can find a detailed description of each one in Hall's "The Ancient Ruins of Rhodesia". There's also a simple, but informative map accompanying the text. Field research has determined that only four are prominent, the rest are minor fortifications.

Historically, Khami is thought to have been the capital of a gold mining district. Large debris fields are found throughout the ruins (some exceed fifteen feet in depth) suggesting at times the population was considerable. Copper, bronze and iron objects as well as glass beads and soapstone pipes have been found at the site. Shards of pottery can be found by the score. Forty ounces of gold in the form of wire, beads and other small objects were recovered by adventurers Neal and Johnson. Early excavations revealed several layers of pavements (this is a common feature amongst the oldest Zimbabwe ruins).

The masonry used in building the structures is cut from granite. However, blocks of diorite (dark gray coarsely grained igneous rock) are worked into the constructions from time-to-time. All four styles of Zimbabwe masonry can be found in the ruins. Check patterns abound throughout the site, but the herring bone pattern can be seen too.

At a big sign that read Green Gables, Peter turned right onto a dirt track and then drove towards a group of low hills. Soon, tall grasses closed in along the edge of the road, making it like a chasm. When a circular wall formed up along the left side, I told him to pull over.

"Here?" He asked.

"Yes!" I yelled, as the adrenaline surged through my body. Before the car had fully stopped, I was out of the door and charging the objective.

The semi circle wall was a yard in height, give or take a few feet here and there. The courses are irregular. On one end, the wall butts up against a group of boulders. Where, after a pronounced curve inwards, the stones are skillfully melded against the larger rock (here they appear uniform in size). On the other end, the wall rounds into the hillside where the masonry is crumbling away or concealed by dirt and vegetation. Two rows of diorite are layered in near the bottom, mid-way along the wall.

Jumping back into the taxi, we drove a little further and then stopped near a small building. Though marked museum, it was nothing more than the shack where they took the money; it cost ten bucks to get in. Signs led to a flight of widely spaced rock steps that gave way to a saddle and a series of lightly wooded hills.

Immediately to the right a low wall wavered along until meeting with some big rocks (there is a squared doorway just prior to them); they seem intentionally set in the ground. The wall continues between them. Two rows of check pattern, three courses each, run the entirety up to the door. The checks continue between the rocks too.

Up ahead is the bulk of Khami. It consists of five ellipses spread out in a line. A gully is on one side and a two hundred foot drop is on the other. Three of them, called the "A", "B" and "C" plateaus are built so close they could be a single conglomeration. Passage ways and steps link them together and lead to various elevations within the site. Huge boulders have been worked in with the construction and there are a number of walls that join at right angles, indicative of one of the later periods. Overall, there is an organic flow to the place and the check pattern abounds throughout the ruins.

From the hill tops the works appear disheveled; fields of stones lay about. In some parts, sections of wall have crumbled away.

In other areas, they have been restacked. The courses fluctuate between slightly uniform to greatly irregular. From the gully, the terraces come into full view and appear monumental, like grand steps ascending the ridgeline.

The façade at the C-plateau is the most impressive. Here, there are seven terraces tapering up and back, conforming to the slope of the hill. Almost every wall is adorned with the check pattern; the highest levels have the best examples. Midway, there are two rows of cord pattern that terminate at a massive boulder. It's lodged in on the right side of the masonry. Along the bottom terrace, a row of checks comes to an abrupt stop and the size and shape of masonry changes noticeably.

Two more ellipses/terraces lie just beyond the "ABC" plateau. On the first, there is a large rock at the top where small stones have been arranged into a cross. Originally, it is thought that Jesuit missionaries assembled the stones sometime between the years 1560-1750. However, as more and more visitors came to Khami, the stones were pulled away for various reasons. The newest ensemble is accompanied by loads of coins. The last ellipse is mostly obscured by long grasses, but the part that's exposed has some interesting features. The top of the wall, at least what's left of it, appears to be the remains of three rows of check pattern with two rows of diorite worked in between them.

Finally, across the gully there is another small site on top of a hill, but there's hardly anything left, just a sparse foundation roughly twenty feet in diameter. It's thought to have been a fort.

By chance, there was a school field trip under way. Small groups of teenage boys and girls dressed in red t-shirts and green track suits (probably the school colors) surveyed the grounds. When a pair of girls made directly for me, I hovered off to the side waiting for them to pass.

"Sir, I'd like to make a picture," one of them said, and then held up her mobile phone.

"Sure," I responded, thinking she wanted to imbibe the spiritual enlightenment of the panoramic view; scrubby lowlands and rocky hills tapered off into the distance while puffy clouds sailed overhead.

"No sir. We want a picture with you," she said, and then signaled to her pal.

"No problem," I smiled, though a bit surprised by her request.

Before we'd finished, a few more students queued up behind them. Then, they came in droves, each one pulling out their mobile phones and asking for a group photo with me.

In an amusing way, I wondered why the kids took an interest. Was it the clothes? I'd been sporting a set outfit for all the ruins; a white shirt, and khaki pants or shorts, all cut from linen. A collapsible straw hat was cinched down on the grape and I was still tracking in my Gilligan's Islands. This time I wore long sleeves with shorts. The mama at Packers ironed them up nice and crisp. She even called me "Doctor!" right before leaving.

Back down at the museum, I asked the attendant about the rest of the ruins. "Where are the other parts? Khami consists of eleven different sites, right?"

She gave me a perplexed look and then responded, "I'm not sure, but there is one more. Pass there and you'll see a gate. Don't go out. Just go right and watch for the green arrows."

Following her directions, I headed down into the dip marked picnic area. While the school chaperones were busy running the grill pit (man, the food smelled great!), the kids had fragmented into small groups. The thought of exercising my photo buddy credentials for a free plate was on my mind, until something caught my eye.

Atop a rocky hill directly ahead there was another low scale wall, this one consisting of two styles of masonry. The bulk of it matched the prevailing stone work found throughout, but the second part was lowest quality I'd seen so far. In fact, it wasn't even properly faced, odd shaped rocks merely wedged together and wavering badly.

At the fence gate, green arrows were painted on rocks. They pointed to a trail running through the woods, across massive boulders and up to a big dam. That's where the arrows forked into two different directions, but after snooping around a set of large boulders I found a narrow passage.

On the other side, the trail fed down into a small, but heavily eroded stone wall enclosure. It's the shape of a box with a square door opening to a small body of water. A huge rock has been incorporated into the plan just like in other parts of the Khami ruins. Outside the door to the immediate left are the remains of a significant structure. Originally, it was a two tiered wall 200 feet long and 27 feet high. There were also three rows of check pattern running along the top, but things have changed. Now only the top tier can be seen. The nearby dam has created a reservoir that obscures the bottom tier. The top layers of the wall have been shaved away so that only two rows of check remain. All of the stone work is clean and tightly fitted.

They said Khami was used as a gold smelting center and a regional capital. Considering the number of out forts, this could be true. However, when reflecting upon the "ABC" plateau it seems more like a ceremonial gathering spot. With a little thought, it's easy to see massive bon fires and throngs of dark sweaty bodies heaving with that special rhythmic unison that Africans have. On the platforms overhead stands a big chief, a council of tribal elders or a high priestess of the darkest order.

XXVI

The Dorm

In Zimbabwe, the mini busses are called Combis and come with wagons latched onto the back. The one I rode in had a high roof and several seats to spare. The driver sped along maintained roads with sparse amounts of traffic. The landscape had a gentle pitch to it and kopjes (small rocky hills) dominated the environment. Despite repetitive check points we made it to Masvingo in just under four hours. Here I would visit the best known ruins in sub-Saharan Africa.

Great Zimbabwe consists of three complexes: the Hill Ruins, the Temple and the Valley Ruins. Previously referred to as the Acropolis, the Hill Ruins are built into a collection of castellated boulders atop a 500 foot high kopje. It overlooks the entire complex. The Temple, the grandest of all Zimbabwe ruins, is a massive elliptical 289 feet in length, 35 feet tall and 16 feet thick at the base. Finally, the maze of wrecked and disheveled structures between the two aforementioned sites is called the valley complex. All three are built from blocks of granite (nearly uniform in size) cut from nearby kopjes. Like other Zimbabwe constructions of the first period, the courses here are mortarless too.

At the National Camp Ground, I landed accommodations in the dorm for twelve bucks a night. The camp had four buildings total, a men's and a ladies' dorm, a BBQ hut and an outhouse with showers (those showers were the hottest yet!). The compound was boxed in with a chain link fence to keep out the wild animals, but the gate always swung open. Considering I had the whole place to myself, it wasn't a bad deal. Some staff members had a room in the other building, but during the day, the place was empty. Mosquitoes weren't a problem, but the cock roaches were streaming all over the place. The first night wave-after-wave assaulted my position, one even breaking through the lines and biting me on the ear. In retaliation, I fired up a mosquito coil and gassed them out.

The place's only dilemma was no food or beverages anywhere nearby. So, the first night I was forced to patronize a fancy hotel with a mock-up of the Great Zimbabwe tower by the front gate. A three egg omelet was eight bucks and 500 ml jugs of water were two bucks each. If you think that's bad, the all you can eat buffet cost twenty-six bills (talk about getting harpooned!).

The next morning I headed back towards town, tossing my thumb at the first vehicle passing by. A small pickup truck slowed and the window rolled down.

"You're still walking," the passenger said in a jovial way.

"Hmmmm," I mumbled, and then wondered what he was talking about.

"We greeted you earlier today," the driver added. "You were walking near the gate."

Prior to trekking up the hill I passed by the guard shack and vaguely remember saying "hi" to a small group of people.

"Hey, are you guys gonna give me a ride or what?" I said with a smile, hoping to get a lift.

"Of course," the passenger said.

"How much," I asked, because the going rate was two bucks into town.

"For free, don't worry."

"What?"

"Just get in!" The driver shouted, in a jovial way.

Alfred, the passenger, and Paul, the driver, were both employed by a firm that supplied oxygen to Zimbabwe's medicinal services industry. Alfred was a sales manager and Paul was the engineer who demonstrated the equipment.

"We're getting the word out," Alfred announced enthusiastically. "But things are a bit slow now."

"So," Paul asked. "How are you finding Zimbabwe?"

"Guys, can I be frank here?" I asked.

"Most certainly," Alfred responded while Paul shook his head in agreement.

"I've seen lots of sites, the weather is nice and you know what, everybody is really-really friendly."

"Welcome. Welcome," both men nodded appreciatively.

"How far have you come," Paul asked.

In a brief summarization, I told them about the ruins in Ethiopia, meeting my buddy in Kenya, visiting the islands in Tanzania and the bus ride to Harare. I even shelled out a few details about my time with Atieno.

Alfred's eye brows arched skyward. Paul braked suddenly and then leaned over the steering wheel and spoke in a very stern voice. "Now I want to confirm, was it just the cooking you were getting, or was there something else going on?"

"My friends," I said in a very pronounced way and then tossed out two thumbs up.

"That is so nice," Alfred commented as a massive smile spread across his face.

By now, Paul was smiling too. "He did well!"

"Yes, yes!" Alfred said, while his head nodded up and down.

"In fact," Paul began, and then jabbed his index finger into the air. "I'm surprised you even left her place, because if it were me, getting away might have been very difficult!"

By far, these two were the coolest blokes I'd met yet. A fitting end to the story would have been a couple of drinks at a roadside joint topped up with more stories, but they were already late for their first appointment.

"Next time," they both chuckled and then sped down the road after dropping me off at a Spar mini-mart. There, I stocked up with three days worth of provisions and then hitch-hiked back to the ruins.

XXVII

Great Zimbabwe

Amongst the entire Great Zimbabwe complex there are two places of note; the Hill Ruins and the Temple. Deciding which site to look at first wasn't easy. As far as the crow flies, the Hill was closer, but when considering the elevation and effort it takes to get to the top, a bit further. Before starting the tour I dug a Kenyan 40 bob Shilling coin out of my bag of sensitive items and flipped it, heads for the Hill and tails for the Temple.

When ascending the Hill, there are a couple of routes to choose from, each with varying difficulty. For a deeper spiritual experience, take the ancient one (it's the hardest). At first the steps are broad, easy and follow the slope of the hillside, but they tighten up significantly at the first bend. Then, the route gets steeper with each step. Soon, stone walls form up on both sides of the path like a trench. They funnel you through a massive rock with a huge split in it. There's no relief in the confines, the narrow path just gets steeper. Trudge a little further and that last flight of steps will thrust you onto the face of the ruins.

Standing over thirty feet tall the main wall is monolithic in appearance. Four towers, each over a yard tall, sit on top (there used to be seven). A narrow passage in the front wall leads into the fortress. Keep your head tucked nice and low until all the way through or you'll get clipped. Inside, there's a courtyard with a nice view of the valley ruins and the Temple. When the first explorers arrived they discovered huge monoliths and large pillars of soap stone (a soft metamorphic rock easily shaped or carved). Some believed they were set in place to make solar and celestial observations.

Immediately, your curiosity will be drawn towards the narrow slot at the back of the courtyard; it leads deeper into the complex. There, millions upon millions of flat rocks have been melded into towering walls that flow and weave around colossal boulders. Keep to the right and follow the contours of that massive boulder. Fit through the smallest of openings and then you'll come to the back lot. Just push a wee bit more and you'll notice an obscure trail that leads up through an inconspicuous opening.

Keep your head low, move forward, and then pivot to the right twice. After a bit of high stepping the trail tops out on a big flat rock (like a roof). You've reached the high point. Now's a time to kick back for a couple of biscuits and a refreshing slug of bottled water (you'll need it after the climb).

The word "complex" is the best way to describe this place. With exception to the main entrance and the courtyard, the rest of the position is a maze of narrow passageways and open spots (one of the earliest explorers called it a labyrinth). The initial fun of visiting comes in wandering around and seeing where you end up (though after a couple of laps you'll be able to terrain associate quite easily). Still, at some point you'll want to find a map and see how the masonry blends in with the rocky environment from overhead.

Early on these ruins were known as "the Acropolis" (a fortified city). As you make several revolutions through the site you'll see why: every crack, crevice and rock overhang is worked into the architecture, creating choke points that restrict the flow of movement. Hi-jacking this setup is a suicide mission. With the slightest appraisal, it's easy to imagine the attackers getting gored with a spear, subject to piping hot liquids pouring down from above or victim to a hail of poison tipped arrows.

Once you're fueled back up, take a look out into the valley. You can see the rest of the ruins afar and the hilltops rippling back into the horizon. After spying the Temple, you'll want to check it out, but before you head back down, there's another spot to see. Find your way to the side of the kopje that faces the valley. There, you'll experience another set of massive walls at the edge of the cliff (its 90 feet high).

While admiring the endeavor, you might notice a dark opening slightly obscured by some scruffy brush. There's just enough of a gap to make out the workings of men (more stacked stone). Follow the narrow trail that skirts the rock overhang (it leads to the grotto), but watch out for the caretaker, he might be shuffling about directly overhead. So, your advance must be surreptitious. Once inside the cave you'll find stone blocks stacked up the same way as above, but layered with dust, lichens and dried moss. The place seems untouched since the first explorers came through over a hundred years ago. Gazing into the shadowy confines will have you wondering if this is a tomb or a vault holding the last cache of gold ingots.

Circling back through the maze of passageways, I found a lofty perch right above the courtyard. There, I began to ponder the events and activities that may have transpired through the centuries, but my solitude was quickly broken by a group of children and an attractive woman entering the courtyard. Without hesitation, they strode right up to my position.

"Hi there," I said, to the woman.

"Hello," she replied. "From where do you come?"

"States. Ohio."

"How do you find Zimbabwe?" she asked.

"The weather is great and the people are friendly," I replied, with a patented answer, though I genuinely meant it. So far the people I met in Zimbabwe were some of the nicest I'd seen along the tour.

She smiled back, but did not speak. Though her warm eyes suggested she was open to more conversation.

"So, are you the...ah..." I paused slighty. "...the mother here?"

"That one is my sister, my small sister, my brother and this is my son," She smiled proudly, and then pointed to a little tyke with an inquisitive look.

"So, you took the ancient route up, yeah?"

"Yes, and now I need to rest," she panted and then dabbed at her temple with a white hanky. "I'm tired."

"Well, I know a place you can lay down," I said.

Her eyes glowed and smile spread across her face. "What is that?"

"It's just over there, in the back. There's a secret hide out up in the rocks. You can take a nap and no one will know."

"Ah!" Sweet mother said, with a bit of amusement.

"Come on, funsters. Let's go!" I said, and then led the posse back into the maze.

Rounding the curves we arrived at the back lot. "Okay, you see that trail to the doorway? On the other side there's a secret room."

Erupting into a chorus of giggles, the children charged forward. Mother dabbed her forehead with the hankie again and then looked back and smiled. Having fulfilled my obligations as a ruins guide, I found my way out through the back way, passing more massive walls (in a disheveled state) and then headed back down towards the Temple.

Back in the valley, I made a brief stop in the museum (home to the famed Zimbabwe birds). My interest in these sculptures is not so great, but they may come into play at a site further south across the border. So, I'll give you their story. Essentially they are bird profiles crudely carved from soapstone. Originally, they were mounted on top of a three foot long shank (all one piece of soapstone). During the era of exploration, pillage and plunder, souvenir seekers hacked them free of the perches and carted them off to separate destinations. Now, they sit in a display case.

The birds have come to be an iconic symbol that represents Zimbabwe. They were also used in seals and symbols for Rhodesia too (the name of the house while under minority rule). In his book "The Lost City of Solomon & Sheba: An African Mystery" Robin Brown-Lowe states there may be a relation to Horus. The symbol of the ancient Egyptian sun god is a hawk.

After surveying the other artifacts in the museum, I headed to the Temple, passing through the valley ruins and intersecting a troop of baboon along the way. To the uninitiated these are cute little buddies, but the reality is they are thieves of the first order. They will carry away any and everything that isn't nailed down. Closing in, I signaled them to clear off, but they wouldn't budge. Extending the monopod for my camera to its full length, I brought it up to my shoulder like a rifle and then made a bayonet charge on the biggest animal. "Yeaaaaaaaaaaaaaaahhhhhhhhhhhh!"

They broke ranks and quadruple timed it to the tree line, a brown furry wave washing across the pitch. Once higher up, they started mouthing off. So, I cocked that monopod back over my shoulder like a spear; the mere gesture sent the lot of them high tailing it deeper into cover.

Adam Renders, an American adventurer, is credited as the first man of European heritage to have seen the ruins. By

1871 he'd been living on the doorstep of the site for several years. His story is not well known, but it's said he'd been a sailor before going native. Eventually, he settled in with the Shona people and took the village headman's two daughters as wives. Renders was followed by a succession of adventurers; Carl Mauch, a German geologist, visited with Renders help in 1871-72. Our friend Bent (from Ethiopia) made his appraisals in 1891 and an Englishman, John Willoughby, conducted extensive mapping of the ruins in 1892. However, it's quite possible that the Portuguese stumbled upon the site first. You can find Portuguese maps of southern Africa with a place called "Simbaoe" on them.

The first reports from the field indicated that Great Zimbabwe was in total disarray. The massive walls were crumbling and it was overgrown with trees hundreds of years old. The open spaces were littered with the stuffs of human and animal occupation. Word is some of the first adventurers spent weeks clearing away the tangles of vegetation so to get proper access to its interior. These days the grounds are kept nice and tight (a grass cutter pushed a mower the entire time I was there).

The best way to see the Temple is to start at the square opening called the West Entrance, but don't go in, swing wide to the right and absorb the magnitude of the place. As you round along the back side, drift out ten to twenty meters and then look up. See the double row of chevrons way up high, pretty neat. Now, look in a little deeper and check out those small rocks holding them in place and then think about this. All the work: finding the stone, quarrying the stone, cutting the stone, carrying the stone and then fitting that stone intricately into place so it stays standing for a thousand years. See the gravity of it all?

Let's take a minute and look at some logistics and think about the numbers. Completing this task required laborers of some sort (most likely press ganged or conscripted). There were also craftsmen, overseers and engineers present. These people required housing, food and clothing. Imagine the undertaking it took to keep this all in motion.

Rounding the other side of the temple brings you to the outer passage. It's short because you're hanging a left at the curvy steps and sneaking in through the North Entrance. Stay left, sharp left, and then cruise along the inner passage way. A tall interior wall mirrors the outer wall. As you advance further into the passage it tightens up and then gets cool and dank; even spiritual for a moment. After transcending the choke point it opens back up. You pass through a doorway and emerge near the great tower, but the view is blocked by a tree. So, keep tracking around to the left. Once you've passed the massive stone column, turn around and check out the girth of it.

Comprised of the same stone as the walls, the tower stands thirty feet tall and has a diameter of fifteen feet at the base and eight at the top. Its actual purpose is unclear, but some say it has religious significance while others claim that it symbolizes a Karanga grain bin. Despite its unique presence, there are a couple of artifacts from fields afar that share its appearance. In Zanzibar, there is a minaret with a chevron built into its side. Also, an ancient coin from the Phoenician town of Byblos has a tower on it that is similar in shape and form.

After sizing up that massive cone, you're caught in the pocket, but there are two ways out. Straight takes you into the courtyard where you can continue your appreciation of the temple walls. Or, you can hang a right and then meander through the inner enclosures (also known as the platform area). Just like their brethren up on the hill these walls are organic, curving around in a circular motion like an eddy in a stream. Either way you run, you'll end up on the other side of the Temple where you can snake out through that massive V-cut in the wall. Afterwards, take a relaxed position on steps, survey the interior and then reflect on the Temple's origins.

The official narrative, known as the Shona school, states that Great Zimbabwe is the work of Karanga natives "during recent times". This conclusion was drawn by an archaeologist named David Randall-McIver in 1899 after a five month tour of seven major sites. It's a peculiar assessment when the observations shared by the first explorers stated the indigenous population had no knowledge of the builders. Nor did they have any understanding of the value of gold-taking a preference to copper ornamentation instead.

On the contrary, the Romantic school suggests that the structures are the mark of a Mediterranean or Arabian race and their quest for gold (some thought it was Ophir). Our friend Bent made the following statement after completing his work: "a race coming from Arabia- a race which spread more extensively over the world than we have at present any conception of, a race closely akin to the Phoenicians and the Egyptians, strongly commercial, and eventually developing into the more civilized races of the ancient world".

Personally, I find the Shona school a tad simple. Here's why: in my hometown there is a section of the city called "Over-the-Rhine". A hundred years ago, it was a thriving community built by German immigrants. As the descendents of the Fatherland moved out the spaces were occupied by the descendents of slaves. As time passed, this section of town fell into decline. If you were to apply the Shona logic in this neighborhood during the mid-eighties to early nineties would it mean that the buildings and streets had been built by the descendents of slaves? No! That said the current occupiers are not necessarily the builders.

By now you're probably thinking that I'm a proponent or supporter of the Romantic School. If so, you're absolutely right. It's because the massive elliptic of the Temple is not unique to Zimbabwe. In fact, in southern Arabia there is another site very similar in design. It's called Awwam. In ancient times it was known as "Ilumqah" or the Temple of the Moon (sound familiar?). There's not a lot of information on this site. Considering the hostilities breaking out in Yemen, there may not be for some time. However, there are pictures showing a kidney shaped formation poking above the Arabian sands. Though heavily eroded, the walls are still nine meters high in some places. In close up photographs the masonry appears refined and similar in dimension to the Sabaen ruins in Ethiopia. Excavations commenced in 1951, but were stopped due to the "dangerous times".

To further our examination of the two structures, open a couple of Internet browsers and then go to Google Maps. Next, do a search for Great Zimbabwe in the first window and a search for Awam Tempel in the second. Once you've arrived on location adjust the imagery until both ruins fill the screen equally. Now, compare the two by toggling back and forth between the windows. In general, the form and structure of the main element (the elliptical) is very similar; it's referred to as "oval kidney shape". The specific substructures vary; the interior of Great Zimbabwe has more circular structures while Awwam has a box temple built into one side. In the chapter "The Gold of Ophir" of Brown-Lowe's book, there is a chart comparing the two sites. The construction, plan, orientation and dimensions of Great Zimbabwe and Awwam are very similar. It's probably safe to say they are related.

Finally, we can argue back and forth between the two schools all day long, but the discussion could probably be settled once and for all through contemporary science. As noted before, skeletons of the "ancients" have been removed from 1st period Zimbabwe ruins. Currently, they're probably boxed up and forgotten in an Indiana Jones style repository, but an inventory of old storage facilities may yield what we're looking for. If located, the remains can be subject to DNA testing. Imagine the reaction if its proven that Africa is a little bit more racially diverse than people want to admit. Would academic institutions and media outlets embrace such a result or would the information be snuffed out by the Cult of Political Correctness?

XXVIII

The Outpost

While in Zimbabwe I had planned on visiting three different ruins. Great Zimbabwe, Khami and another site, hopefully further off the track. In preparation, I'd made a copy of a map included with Nicklin-Hall's "The Ancient Ruins of Rhodesia". The names of the ruins are plotted in red ink all over the map, with a high density north of Gwanda, a small town south-east of Bulawayo. But, before I jaunted off, I touched base with a couple of authorities in search of directions. The first stop had been the Bulawayo National Museum where I met with one of the archaeologists.

"Yes, there are other ruins," he began. "But I'm not sure exactly where. There's an older archaeologist who knows, but he's gone right now."

"Will he be back tomorrow?" I asked, excited at the potential lead.

"No, he's out of the country."

Great, I thought, and then headed off to the Tourist Information Center further into town. In the cramped quarters of the bureau, I showed a woman my map. She gave it a quizzical glance and then went to rummage around in the back.

"I think this is what you're looking for," she said upon returning, and then handed me a copy of "Zimbabwe, Africa's Paradise" a glossy tourist brochure that profiled the country's major attractions.

Not quite, but it had been worth a try. So, I continued trawling around the city streets and finally ended up at a second hand shop called Vigne Books. An older gent of European heritage ran the place He seemed interested in my quest. So, I spread the map out across the top of a glass counter and he gave it a look.

"Oh, yes," the proprietor began. "This is actually based on an older map which I believe was produced in the late 1800's.

"See those ruins," I said, and then pointed at the names in red ink listed above Gwanda. "I want to visit them."

"Well, I'm very familiar with the region south of Gwanda," he stated. "I can assure you, there are no ruins down there. However, north of Gwanda, I'm not so sure."

"So, there could still be ruins?"

"Possibly, but you're facing two problems. First, you don't have your own vehicle, and second, if the ruins are still there, they'll be completely overgrown with vegetation," he replied.

So, there it was. The brutal honesty of heading down to Gwanda in search of lost cities was a crapshoot. I could hire a guy to drive me around for a few days, work on some villagers and maybe get lucky. Then again, I could blow a boat load of cash and come up empty handed. At that point, holding off on field operations was the best plan, at least until I got to Great Zimbabwe. Surely someone at the biggest archaeology site in Southern Africa would know what's going on. During that brief stop at the Great Zimbabwe museum, I ran it by the curator.

"They are just small ruins," she said, dismissing the less known sites as if they had little significance.

"Who cares if the ruins are small?" I replied. "There could be a unique design in the masonry, or even better, experiencing the thrill and excitement of discovery."

But no matter how many times I stressed their significance, she dismissed the locations as if there was really no reason to check them out.

With three strikes and an incomplete under my belt, I crossed off the field operation. Not because there wasn't something of merit to rediscover (there had to be), but the time and money would be an issue. It was time to make a decision- continue on to South Africa with only two in the bag, or double back and check out a third site. There were signs between Shangani and Bulawayo for a handful of ruins tucked off the main road. So, it might be worth a try.

At seven the next morning I was flagging down a Combi for a lift back into Musvingo. By eight-thirty, I was on a ZUPCO bus muscling its way out of town. Once on the open road, a woman dressed completely in red, including a big floppy hat, stood in the aisle and started wailing, singing and then chanting over-and-over like she was warding off the devil. In a way it was interesting, at least until the driver jumped in on it. First, it was just weird hand signals, but then he snapped his head around and eye balled the lady, oblivious to oncoming traffic. When the driver finally looked back at the road, he bounced up and down in his seat and popped side-to-side like he was break dancing. Showtime faded out once we hit the hills and that metal crate climbed up to Gweru.

As the hours passed, I weighed the numbers and saw a one hundred dollar day (meals, travel costs and entry fees) looming ahead. With the time looking funny and the money stacking up, would it be worth it? Momentarily, the eject button flashed through my mind, but what for? The whole reason for this trip was to visit ruins. If the daily cost ran up, I was still saving in the long run.

By the time the driver pulled into the terminus and threw it into park, it was high noon. Getting to the ruins would take at least another forty-five minutes, and that was after organizing a ride. So, there was no time for delays.

Outside the bus station, I signaled the first taxi driver I saw.

"Yes," an older gent with a pot belly and a receding hair line acknowledged, as he shut the door on a compact vehicle. It had snap-on micro wheels and safety straps holding the hubcaps in place.

"Can we organize?" I asked, while glancing down at my watch.

"Where to?" He replied.

"Nanatale ruins, down by Shangani. Do you know the place?"

"I do."

"How much to take me down there, give me thirty minutes at the site and then bring me back so I can catch a combi to Musvingo?"

"I'll have to check," he answered, and then dialed out on his mobile. "Just give me a moment."

After a brief conversation he hung up.

"What did they say?" I asked, eager to get rolling.

"I'm still checking," he responded, pointing one finger up and signaling for extra time.

"I don't have all day, buddy. How about a flat rate, say fifty bucks?"

"Just let me talk to someone," he pleaded, and then chatted up another driver.

After a few moments, he stepped back to the curb. "Ok, it's good."

"You're sure?" I asked, and then confirmed the arrangement. "Fifty bucks up, a half hour there and then back, right?"

"Yes, we can go."

Awesome, I thought, and then slide into the back of the taxi.

"But if you don't mind," he added. "My wife will come too."

Just then, a woman several months pregnant and cradling a large fruit sat down in the front passenger seat. Now, I wasn't opposed to her coming along, but I thought it worth a try to have her chip in a bit.

"You want to throw in ten bucks?" I asked nonchalantly.

"No," she laughed. "But I'll share my water melon with you."

"Ah, that's ok."

As we spun out of town, we made our introductions and then discussed the bus ride up.

"So, Mr. Eric," Louice, the driver's wife, began. "From where did you start today?"

"Masvingo," I replied. "And the coolest thing was passing all those gold mines." There had been signs to a half dozen mining operations along the way.

"Those places are producing very much gold," said Thomas, the driver.

"Yes," agreed Louice. "And there are diamonds around here too, but most are near Mutare."

It's been reported that Zimbabwe is one of the world's top diamond producing countries. Diamonds are a clear and extremely hard carbon based mineral that form roughly one hundred miles deep in the earth's mantle. Rock containing diamonds rise to the surface via volcanic pipes. From time-to-time massive alluvial fields are discovered in the country's eastern region near Mozambique.

"You've come at a good time," Louice said. "Back in 2008, it was very difficult."

"You mean the hyperinflation?" I said, more so confirming than asking.

Once one of the strongest economies in Africa, Zimbabwe has come under hard times. Back in 2008 things were dire. Somehow, the central government thought printing currency at staggering denominations would fix the problem. They even came up with a 100 trillion dollar note (these days they go for about ten-to-twelve bucks a pop on Ebay), but this only led to people scraping up boat loads of cash just to acquire life's basic necessities, like bread and milk. Soon after, the Zimbabwe dollar was outlawed.

With the crash of Zimbabwe's economy, the Chinese African Empire came riding in and worked sweet deals on natural resources so that Africa's breadbasket would starve no more. Now, the shelves are stocked again and the US dollar is the main currency (they're even circulating two dollar bills), the coinage comes back in South African Rand.

"Can you believe the shelves were empty?" Thomas chimed in, while glancing up at the rear view mirror.

"There was nothing!" Louice exclaimed. "We would queue in the morning to buy food. Hours would pass. When we got to the end, the store only had beer, every time!

"Then how did you guys survive?"

"If you had people abroad, they could wire money to Mozambique, Botswana or South Africa," Thomas said, this time glancing back over his shoulder. "Then, we bought our groceries and just came back."

"So, you two have been to South Africa? I'm heading there next.

"You're going to South Africa?" Louice said cautiously, and then angled back and looked at me square in the face as best she could. "Don't talk to anyone, but the police. They are all criminals down there, blacks and whites. Bad people can follow you on the bus just to steal money, no matter where you're going."

"It's true," Thomas said adamantly, and then balled up his fist and shook it mightily. "Take care with the money. Roll it! Roll it tightly in your hand and let no one see it when you pay."

The conversation died down and we enjoyed an interlude of country music until passing a sign for the Nanatale turn off. Thomas wheeled to the left and steered onto an old tractor road.

Early on we passed a couple of farms, but soon the acacia trees thickened up and closed in. Every once in awhile a pair of baboons or antelope jogged across the road and disappeared into the dense vegetation.

"Man, we're in the bush now!" I said excitedly, as we closed in on the ruins, but neither one of them heard me. That's because Thomas was running it hard down the road, no brakes and no angles on the ruts, just bulldozing straight ahead. The dashboard shook violently and the plastic on the steering column rattled loose and fell to the floor. Every time we bottomed out, which was with alarming frequency, rocks pelted the undercarriage. Twice, the drive shaft got bulls eyed so hard that that piss ant taxi rang like a bell.

As we rolled on and on, the ride became excruciating. It wasn't even my car, but I grimaced painfully whenever the metal below my feet grated across the high points in the road. The further we went, the more concerned I became, fearing a punctured gas tank or one of the tires blowing out, but the old man didn't even flinch. When we came to a stream or creek he just hit the gas, plowing ahead with such force the water squirted through the holes in the floor boards like tiny geysers.

Finally, we ran up on a collection of ramshackle huts with a faded sign that said "Nanatali Ruins".

"This is it," Thomas said, and then slowed the taxi to a stop.

After getting out, he walked up to one of the shacks, spoke with someone lingering in the shadows and then came back.

"The curator is sleeping," Thomas informed us. "But he's coming."

"When?"

"Just short time," he responded.

The sun was on the down swing and there wasn't time to waste while this guy jacked around. So, I had to make a move.

"Which way to the ruins?" I asked Thomas.

"Just here," he replied, pointing to a narrow trail that began after a rusty barbed wire fence.

"Tell that guy I'll be at the top," I said, and then started off.

After the fence, the trail worked its way through the brush, up a narrow trail and then across a massive rock streaked with veins of quartz. Reaching the top of the kopje, I breached a second round of barb wire and then came face-to-face with the ruins. The late afternoon sun illuminated the masonry in a warm glow.

Nanatale is often cited as the most attractive ruins in the country. That's because you can find four examples of the Zimbabwe stone patterns worked into the outer wall; chevrons, herring-bone, chessboard and cord. Additionally, that same front wall has been reworked into the form of castellated battlements. This modification is thought to have been made well after the fourth period Zimbabwe style, possibly by Portuguese adventurers. At the turn of the 20th century there were still small monoliths mounted atop the battlements.

Sitting on top of a massive granite rock the ruins give way to spectacular views of all four points of the compass. Any invasion force, brigands or marauding band will set off the alarms well before arrival, allowing the inhabitants to implement defensive measures and protect their gold.

Ninety by seventy feet, the ruins are elliptical in shape. The structure is built from undressed blocks of granite. Despite being a small site, this place has seen a lot of action. Sections of the walls have been disemboweled and the guts spill out into the grass like alluvial flows. Off center in the interior there's a pile of dirt covering more stacked rock. At some point in the past, Nanatale, like many of the Zimbabwe ruins, was filled in with dirt by an unknown people.

I had made it to the back side of the ruins when I heard a guy yell, "Hey!"

Near the front, a stocky guy with mirrored sunglasses and his shirt collar pressed shoulder-to-shoulder waved like I was supposed to circle back. This went on for a few minutes. When he figured out I wasn't going to budge, he made tracks in my direction.

"I am the curator," he announced boisterously.

"Right," I said, cutting him off mid-sentence. "And I'm busy, get it? So, I'll find you when I'm done."

"But you have to pay," he objected.

"I'm going to pay, but when I'm done working."

"But you are supposed to pay before entering the site," he continued, as his protest faded into a whimper.

"I'd have paid you if you weren't sleeping," I said, and then wheeled off in a different direction and resumed my appraisal of the site.

The interior layout is reminiscent of a giant wheel. What's left standing of the inner walls connects the perimeter wall to the mound in the middle. Atop the dirt pile is the crumbled remains of daga huts (buildings made from mud).

In his book "Mediaeval Rhodesia" David Randel-Maciver writes about his work on the site. At the time of excavations, 1905, the daga remains were significant enough to identify both a chief's and witch doctor's residences. Items recovered on the mound include bindings of twisted copper, pieces of iron, including spearheads and a band, and the remains of large elephant tusks.

By the time I had completed the survey, Thomas finally made it up the hill. Pulling a wrinkled hankie from out of his back pocket, he wiped the streaks of perspiration from his forehead and then gave the main wall a looking over.

"Do you want to see the whole site?" I asked, eager to make another lap through the ruins.

"Yes," Thomas replied, "But we should really start back for Gweru."

Down at the bottom of the hill, I paid the curator the ten dollar entry fee and we loaded up for the return trip. Due to her pregnancy, Louice could not make it up to the site. So, as we pulled away, I leaned forward and gave her some words of encouragement, "I hope today's action will rub off on your baby in a good way. Hopefully, he or she will grow up to be a big adventurer!"

It was well into the night when I got back to Musvingo. After grabbing a sack of goodies from the deli at OK Supermarket, I snagged a taxi ride back to the dorms because local transport had ended for the day (twenty-five bucks, geez!).

XXIX

Speculations on the Universe and the Technological Evolution of Mankind

It was my last night at the dorms. Tired and worn down, I eased into a reclining position on a picnic table and looked up. The air was cool and the night time sky was devoid of the glare from the big city lights. Orion hung overhead, but at an angle aligned with the southern hemisphere. Behind the Hunter, layer-upon-layer of stars filled in the black void of space until the galactic plane of the Milky Way Galaxy stretched across the sky.

It is estimated that between one and four billion stars make up the Milky Way, a spiral galaxy consisting of a galactic core and several arms reaching outward from the center. Our solar system can be found in the Orion-Cygnus arm roughly two-thirds the way out from the core. Some scientists estimate that there are one billion planets in the galaxy, with the possibility of 17 million Earth like planets distributed throughout the stars.

Every time I imbibe such a magnificent view, I'm just amazed at the people who still embrace a flat earth mentality. With the galaxy so big and home to so many different planets, the place has to be teeming with life; every planet an oasis in the sea of space, some empty and devoid of life, but others having followed set rules of evolution. There are probably living dinosaurs on a planet somewhere in the galaxy. There are bound to be humans too; different species distributed across the galaxy on what is referred to as "Earth-like worlds" the same way that different races are distributed across continents and archipelagos here on Earth. Sure they may look a little different than us, but in general, their physiology is probably identical: two legs and arms, eyes, nose and mouth and beards or something.

When you think about it, the level of development is probably just as diverse too. There has to be advanced technological societies with the least amount of environmental impact, and people whose highest achievement is a mud-and-stick hut accompanied by a dug-out canoe. Heck, somewhere out there, you might even find the grass roots beauty of a spear-chucking cavewomen still wearing skins.

Through the years, I've initiated such discussions only to be met with ridicule and verbal hostility from the non-thinkers of today's society. These flat-earth types cling to the belief that earth is the only populated planet in the galaxy. Or, as they like to toss out, if there are other people out there, then it would be impossible to communicate or visit with them because the distance between the two points is just too vast.

Under current technology, I agree. The idea of building a massive multi-stage rocket that plows through space to the nearest star is the stuff of Victorian Era fiction, but that's not to say the technological evolution of this planet won't continue. In fact, it's just a matter of the right visionary coming along and organizing exceptionally motivated people. Such a technological achievement may require an industrial system in low earth orbit, where a zero-g manufacturing environment allows for the fabrication of crystals and metallurgy required to construct the components necessary for rapid interstellar transit.

Besides, who knows what level of technology exists in top secret government labs these days. You've heard of Area 51, right? Suppose scientists have already devised an airborne platform that runs on neutrinos. In case you're unaware, neutrinos are subatomic particles emitted by the Sun. They reach Earth in seven seconds by the score. In fact, billions of them are passing through your body as you turn the pages on this book.

Additionally, the Earth's magnetic field is always streaming energy. Scientists have determined that it's low yield, but constant. So, why couldn't someone engineer a device that harnesses and then magnifies the full power of this natural resource? Maybe there all ready is. Do you remember all those funny black triangles flying around the northern hemisphere back in the 1990's?

Finally, since I'm talking about electromagnetic energy I want to say something about the aging process. We all know that proper diet and regular exercise can lead to a long bountiful life, but it doesn't reverse the aging process. Do we even know what causes aging? Scientifically, aging is the breakdown of cells at the atomic level. To get an idea of scale, go to YouTube and look up the video "Powers of Ten". During the second half of the presentation the inner world of the human body is explored at the atomic scale.

Through a series of reverse calculations, we are presented with three hydrogen atoms bundled by electronic forces to a carbon atom. The mass shimmers and vibrates intensely. Is aging when these atomic forces lose their charge? If so, perhaps a fountain of electro-magnetic energy could recharge these atomic particles and give eternal life (of course we'd still have to eat right and exercise). That said, suppose there is a secret society shrouded by layers of bureaucracy and hidden at a classified facility (if they are clever, the government might not even know). It could be a group of scientists who are genetically pure and possesses the technology that allows them to live vibrant lives 100+ years and travel to the moon and other bodies within our solar system.

Now, at this point you're probably wondering; hey E, did you just knock back a couple of short stacks at the corner pub or did someone slip you a pinch of Mother Nature's finest? I can assure you at the time of writing I was fully sober, slightly knackered by the day's travel, but only under the influence of adventure and excitement. So, I'm just prepping you up for the final leg of this journey. The last stop is a small town in South Africa where a guy has some theories that are out of this world!

South Africa: Pyramids of the South

XXX

South, across the Border

Twenty-four hours later I was wedged into the middle seat on the night bus to Pretoria. To the left an old man snored loudly and from time-to-time the young woman on the right chatted things up. A field of stars hung overhead while the full moon illuminated big hills and rocky outcrops along the roadside. Thomas and Loice's warning resonated in the back of my mind, but faded away as the bus cruised south to the border crossing at Beitbridge.

Getting out of Zimbabwe was a breeze. The immigration officers stamped my passport without verifying the mug shot. However, in South Africa traffic was stacked up like in Mombasa. So, the bus driver wheeled it into the oncoming lane and ran hard until the South African border guards yelled, "cut it out!" At the lorry park, each bus was gutted of its passengers and the masses prodded along like farm animals. Reveling in the sound of their own voices, blacks employed by South Africa's Home Office verbally abused everyone entering the country. When travelers didn't line up just as told, their intelligence was brought to scrutiny in the most degrading way.

"Are you stupid?" Angry faces shouted from behind the security of pressed uniforms and orange safety vests.

After a lot of noise we were queued up behind the other herds in the courtyard of a square building. We waited and waited until told to move indoors and then approach a row of windows.

"How long will you visit South Africa?" A stout woman barked through a circular cut out.

"About a week or so," I replied, and then pushed my passport forward underneath the glass.

"And what will you do?" She snapped.

"I'm going to visit some historic sites," I said, slightly put off by her brash demeanor.

"Ok, you have seven days in South Africa," she snarled, and then shoved my passport back under the glass and waved to the next person. Only a week, I thought. Weren't Americans supposed to get ninety days upon entry? We do everywhere else!

Rolling onwards towards Pretoria the night bus stopped time-to-time at a stop-n-go gas station just like in the States. They were brightly lit and fully stocked. The floors freshly mopped and the bright work in the rest rooms highly reflective. At each stop I replenished my supply of beverages and crisps. Despite my stomach roaring thunderously, I refused solid food of any kind, saving my appetite for the final destination.

Back on the road, I drifted back off into the night sky and thought about what was out there. Like many places around the globe South Africa has had its share of UFO sightings. Most involve bright lights and unknown flying objects. There are also reports of strange impressions left in the ground by visiting spaceships and small slant eyed chaps dressed up in metallic coveralls. Aside from these standard observations, South Africa is also home to two fascinating stories: the Elizabeth Klarer Experience and the Kalahari Incident.

The first report involves a young woman who grew up near the Drakensburg Mountains. As chronicled in Rob Marsh's "Unsolved Mysteries of southern Africa" Elizabeth Klarer had her first UFO experience at the age of seven. Late one evening a strange metallic craft intercepted an earth bound meteor and prevented the impact. Her second sighting occurred many years later when she and her husband at the time piloted a small plane from Durban to Jo-burg. Mid-flight, they were intersected by a massive circular craft shrouded in a blue halo.

Two years later Elizabeth ventured to a place called Flying Saucer Hill. There she found a six foot tall man standing next to a large UFO. Akon, as he was called, was part of a scientific exploration team originating from planet Meton. Elizabeth was invited onboard and the craft left Earth to rendevouz with a much larger ship in space. While onboard the mother ship, Elizabeth was shown several presentations about planet Meton, an ocean world orbiting the star Proxima Centuri (a red dwarf just over four light years from our solar system). The Metonions were a telepathic people who were technologically advanced and ecologically in tune with their environment. However, they had a slight problem. As their population was small, they were in dire need of new genetic material to keep their race going. Now here's where it starts to get interesting. It seems that Akon had had his eye on Elizabeth for some time. All those UFO sightings were actually him scoping her out, and for good reason too. You see, Elizabeth had been selected for a breeding project meant to revitalize the Meton race. As you can guess, Elizabeth became pregnant and was taken to the planet Meton to give birth, but the planet's environmental factors were too much. She left after a short stay.

The Metons were also concerned with cultural development of planet Earth and mankind's conflicts with nature. So, they tasked Elizabeth out with enlightening mankind. Upon returning to Earth she wrote a book called "Beyond the Light Barrier". At the time of writing this manuscript, her book could be found on Ebay for around fifteen dollars a copy.

The second incident is a bit more contemporary, having taken place on May 7th, 1989. A UFO traveling at a speed of 5,746 nautical miles was detected by a South African Naval ship. Once entering South African air space, the contact was confirmed by secondary and tertiary radar units in the air and on the ground. Seven minutes into the observation two Mirage jet fighters were dispatched on an interception course. One of the fighters was rigged up with an experimental laser cannon called a Thor II.

At this point, you might be wondering, laser canons and Africa? Keep in mind, during the Cold War Era South Africa was considered a First World country and also had a clandestine nuclear weapons project. The endeavor culminated in a covert test blast on the South Atlantic referred to as "The Vela Incident".

Upon making visual confirmation and transmitting a radio message (it went ignored) the lead jet opened fire with the Thor II. It scored a direct hit! The UFO lost altitude and crashed into the desert wastelands of Botswana. A recovery team found the damaged craft in the bottom of a massive crater.

Once in a secure location, the South Africans pried open the craft and found two aliens. Man, were they pissed! One of them savaged a medic with claw-like mitts. Now, if you thought this could get any stranger, guess what? A secret agency dispatched by the US Government made a deal with the South Africans. Everything was whisked out of the country and transported to the depository of all things alien, Wright Patterson Air Force Base.

XXXI

The Last Bus Ride

Just after sun up, the bus rolled into Pretoria. There was one more leg to cover and organizing with a local company proved problematic: either the bus had already left or they didn't have a direct run to Waterval. However, there was 9 am bus to Nelspruit (a city further out on the N-4, the east-west highway out of Pretoria). It was heading in the right direction, but I still had to negotiate a bit. After a little coercion, the driver agreed to drop me off at the Waterval junction.

Departing early, the bus worked through the morning traffic and made its way to the outskirts of town where the N-4 picked up. Divided by a grassy median, the four lane highway crossed the gently rolling landscape, passed fields of maize and big rolls of hay, reminiscent of the heartland in America. Drivers operated their vehicles within the boundaries of common sense; no one bogarted the shoulder in an attempt to get ahead. Clean and maintained traffic signs, such as Hi-Jacking Area, High Accident Zone and a telephone number to report wild fires, were posted at regular intervals.

It should be noted that South Africa abounds in natural resources and like Zimbabwe to the north, it is also a land of gold. Witwatersrand is home to the largest gold reef deposit in the world (a reef is a stratified deposit found in sedimentary rock). The Witwatersrand Reef has produced over 1.5 billion ounces; half the world's known production. South Africa is also home to world class kimberlite pipes; igneous rock containing diamonds. In 1869, an 83.5 carat specimen, named the Star of South Africa, was discovered in the bush.

By the time signs for Waterval started showing up the N-4 had tightened down to two lanes and the median had disappeared. The road dipped and rose with the increasing change in grades. When the driver hit the brakes at a three-way intersection, I jumped out and followed a downward slope into a river basin. All along, there were signs for the Stone Circle Bistro, my point of contact for the final jaunt on this trip. After crossing over the river I made a sharp left and then marched another 100 meters to the place.

Michael Tellinger has written a number of books about ancient ruins and lost human history. His most popular are "Slave Species of God", "Adam's Calendar", and "Temples of the African Gods". Sometime after my return to the States he released another book called "African Temples of the Annunaki; the Lost Technologies of the Gold Mines of Enki". Enki, loosely translated as "Lord of the Earth", was an ancient Sumerian god.

Most relevant to my journey is the "Temples of the African Gods". In this publication there are over seventy aerial photographs of the stone circles. They are extensive, not so much in size, but in repetition. Some of the ruins sprawl across the landscape like giant stone spider webs. In other images there is a central focal point and then small scale structures radiate outward like a stone tossed into an early morning pond. Sometimes the ruins are intersected by meandering channels contained by stone walls. In a way, these stone ruins are like a massive circuit board embedded into the rolling landscape. In closer studies, there is a reoccurring pattern; a large outer structure filled in with a series of smaller circles or partitions. This arrangement is like a two dimensional illustration of a cell.

Judging by the images in the book the stones used as building material are mostly flat, but sometimes bulky. Overwhelmingly they appear to have been pulled from a water logged environment; their surfaces are smooth and edges rounded. Their dimensions are such that they could be easily set in place with two hands. Occasionally, the repetition of flat stones is interrupted when a larger flat rock is incorporated into the fabric. Set vertically, they may be symbolic of doors or windows. In other instances circular rocks have been placed in the walls. Tellinger says they indicate the direction east. Interestingly, a number of bird stones have been discovered in or near the ruins. Solid at the base, they taper up to a rounded shoulder (perhaps a folded wing) and then end with an elongated neck. Much larger stones, monolithic in proportion, have a presence across the landscape too. They range in height from 3.5 to 5 meters.

Online, Tellinger can be found in numerous interviews. Some are short, fifteen minutes or less. Others run for a couple of hours: in depth discussions about the stone circles, Adam's Calendar, ancient gold mining and the Annunaki.

Through long hours reconnoitering the country side and examining the ruins up close, Tellinger has come up with some pretty fantastic theories. His interpretations of the stone circles are that they were used to harness the Earth's naturally produced energy. These magnetrons, as he calls them, controlled the energy flow required for a massive gold mining operation. This endeavor, engineered by a race called the Annunaki, was going on for 200,000 years before the Great Flood. In one of his interviews, Tellinger describes the Annunaki as a galactic race of beings from the planet Nibiru in need of gold for their home world.

Tellinger goes on to state that there is an Annunaki still among us called Marduk. Through a series of negotiations, he struck a deal with two alien groups, the Draconians and the Reptilians. In return, Marduk got control of Planet Earth and enslaved humanity by creating our dependency on money. Thus, the gold still moves off world.

Tellinger is also a student of Zacharia Sitchen and an ardent supporter of his theories on the Annunaki. Sitchin was a researcher with big ideas regarding the translation of Sumerian clay tablets and alien visitors. Sumer was an ancient civilization centered in present day Iraq. Excavations in this region have yielded cylinder seals that depict large animals (similar to plant eating dinosaurs) and winged devices with people seated in them. Not everyone agrees with Sitchen's theories. Despite his critics, he wrote fifteen books on the subject and they've gone through multiple printings around the world.

The main building at the bistro had a spacious book shop, a rustic dining room with several new age murals and a front deck with chairs and tables. Fresh green lawns gave the place a country club feel; a far cry from the grubby little holes I'd been patronizing on my way down from Ethiopia. A lesser structure was filled with hundreds of stone implements that had been recovered from the countryside. Big aerial shots of the stone circles where tacked up on the walls. Back in the main building, a black girl minding shop said everyone had gone for the day and that I should come back the next morning.

"Where can I get a place to stay?" I asked, hoping to settle in on the cheap.

"Try Steam," she advised. "It's just in town."

Watervale Boven is Afrikaans for before the water fall. It used to be a service stop on the Mozambique rail line. These days it's a destination for trout fishing and rock climbing on the nearby escarpments (escarpments are long cliffs formed by a geologic event that separates two flat areas vertically). The town is saddled in next to the Elands River and big hills loom on the shoulder. Residential streets branching off from the main drag are fitted with small brick homes called "P95s". Internet connectivity was nowhere to be found, but there was a large grocery store, some mom and pop joints and a gas station. Luckily, the local bank took travelers checks. Here, the blacks looked on silently, white children roamed barefoot and the locals whizzed around in small pick-up trucks called Bakkies.

As parochial as it seemed, the place wasn't so far off the track. One night while walking to one of the mom and pop joints, I passed a black man on the street.

"Mzungu, how are you?" He called out, greeting me the same way as the East Africans.

"I'm fine," I replied, but wondered if a Genie from Swahililand had followed me all the way down to South Africa.

Heading back onto the main road, I passed under a rail bridge and then rounded left into town. Luckily, the Steam Bed and Breakfast was just a few meters ahead. The accommodations were in a one-story brick guest house secured behind a tall iron fence. At thirty-five bucks a night, it was a bit on the high side. Being that I was down to my last few hundred bucks, the burn rate was about to kick in hard. However, the place was very clean and had a nice rustic charm to it. In fact, it was the first time I walked around barefoot without worrying about something burrowing into the bottom of my feet!

After settling in, I strolled over to the local pub and ordered a cheeseburger topped with an egg and bacon. It was reinforced with a mountain of crispy golden fries. The food was so good, and I was so hungry, I demolished a second plate faster than the first. Afterwards, a warm can of Black Label beer helped wash it all down. During my stay the Steam Pub became a regular stop. One night, a contingent of locals had a barbeque and made me a stack of Braii Bread (two pieces of bread, tomato, onion, cheese cured with butter and salt and pepper over the fire). In return, I offered to buy them a round of beer, but they refused, on the account they wanted to assure I was having a good time in South Africa.

While squaring up the bill at the bar, a couple of local blokes struck up a conversation. They spoke English in a heavy accent, the way Afrikaans do, and had a no none sense demeanor to go with it.

"Where are you from, man?" A seasoned individual with a graybeard asked.

"States," I answered. "Ohio, to be specific."

"What brings you down south?" A guy with work boots, hi-cut tennis shorts and a burr head inquired.

"I've come to visit Adam's Calendar and the Footprint of God. Have you heard of these sites?

"Yeah, yeah," Graybeard replied nonchalantly. "There are ruins all over here."

"Then you want to speak with Michael?" The dude asked. "I can dial him if you like."

"Sure, if you don't mind?" I replied.

"No problem."

A few moments later he had Michael on the phone, explained there was a visitor who'd like to see the sites and then passed me over his mobile.

"We can organize, Eric," Michael said, "but you'll have to come down to the Bistro tomorrow and meet with Louise. She'll help arrange things."

Louise was his better half. I'd emailed a couple of times on my way down.

"Cheers, Mike!" I replied, and then passed the dude back his phone.

After a swig of beer, I looked at Graybeard and noticed he was wearing a Mine Lab sport shirt.

"So, where are the goods at, buddy?" I asked.

"Are you looking for treasure?" he responded.

"Well, if it jumped up and smacked me in the face, I wouldn't ignore it," I cracked.

Graybeard chuckled hesitantly.

"But with all seriousness, I wrote an article published in Lost Treasure magazine about a DC-3 full of gold and silver bullion. It disappeared over West Africa right after WW II. What kind of stories do you have down here?"

"The Kruger Gold is the biggest," he said. "Personally, I don't think its out there, but there is gold around. That's why I'm here today. I've just picked up some maps for the gold fields near the border with Swaziland."

South African treasure stories are many. So, you may not be familiar with the story of the Kruger Gold. It's over one hundred years old. In the late 1800's, an area called the Transvaal was the highest producer of gold in the world. Being held by the descendents of Dutch adventurers, it was also independent from the British Empire. The crown was not pleased to be cut out from such a large resource. So, a series of quarrels known as the Boer Wars entangled Great Britain with the Transvaal and the Orange Free State.

The difficulties were led by the President of the Transvaal, Paul Kruger, a bulk of a man with a chinstrap beard and a top hat; he's also immortalized on South Africa's best known gold coin, the Kruger Rand. The crown responded by unleashing a column of soldiers on Pretoria, the Transvaal's capital. As the enemy closed in, there was a mad scramble to round up all the loose gold in town and keep it from the invaders. Gangs of battle hardened men loaded wooden crates onto wagons and trains that disappeared into the cool African night. Much speculation has been made as to where the gold went, but the overwhelming opinion is the hoard lay buried somewhere out in the country side. However, not everyone agrees.

Again, referencing "Unsolved Mysteries of Southern African" Rob Marsh writes of a prisoner called Phillipus Swartz. Swartz had a dodgy past and ended up with a murder rap for knocking off a cohort. He didn't beat the charge, but his legal fees were paid in old gold coins by a mysterious man in the dark of the night.

Returning my attention to Greybeard, I asked about his plan, "Are you going for alluvial gold?"

"Yeah," he said.

"Will you pan for it?"

"Hell no!" He bellowed and rolled his hand into a fist and held it up. "I'll use my metal detector and hopefully find a 3k nugget just like this."

"Precious metals are money," I replied. "I've been putting my cash into silver coins and gold mining stocks, you know, because of the Global Financial Crisis."

"It's completely manufactured," Greybeard said defiantly.

"Yeah, but by whom?" I asked.

"The Illuminati or the Rothschilds," the dude announced, rejoining the conversation.

If you're unaware, the Rothschilds are said to be the wealthiest family on earth. It's been estimated the family coffers hold between 500 and 700 trillion dollars. Some claim their tentacles stretch around the world in the form of central banks. Not only do they influence the countries they've established themselves in, but they also control the global money supply. With such financial clout, it's also speculated that they wield a hand in geopolitical events, determining what countries go to war and why. There are also claims they are behind the globalists and the drive for total domination.

"It's the New World Order," Graybeard added. "They're working for a single currency and a one world government. Europe and America will be a single country one day."

By now the bar maid had finished her work. She was a tall woman with dark hair and large observant eyes. Fully aware of our conversation, she crept over and leaned against the back side of the bar.

"Do you believe in the end times?" She asked in a flat monotone voice.

"Not in a biblical sense, but change is on the way," I answered. "Things are shaping up like Orwell's 1984, specifically in regards to the level of today's electronic surveillance. Do you know the government has the power to track your IP address and monitor your online browsing and spending habits?"

"It's the IP address!" The dude echoed boisterously and then held up his mobile. "And they can track you with this phone."

"As long as you're in range of a cell tower and it has GPS capabilities. They'll know your every move. That's just the tip of the iceberg, though. You have to watch what you're doing online, because somebody else might be."

"What do you mean?" Greybeard huffed, somewhat put off by the revelation.

"For instance," I began, in an academic manner. "Suppose you make a post on a message board that catches someone's attention or you send a funny worded email and it sets off a flag. Your IP address will get mapped to a data analyzer. Soon, they, and I mean the minions of the political class, will be checking what websites you're looking at, monitoring your credit card transactions and checking up on the books you're reading."

"Who?" Greybeard charged.

"A Level-1 Analyst employed by the establishment, but that's just the start. After your data is packaged up, it's forwarded on to a Level-2 analyst, that's who you really have to worry about."

"And who are these Level-2 people?" The dude snarled like he was ready to pass out knuckle sandwiches and elbow kebabs.

"They're the state employed psychiatrists who have been indoctrinated in special ways to hate. It's their job to scrutinize your electronic files and determine what you've been up to. If they think you're in opposition to and in conflict with the policies and agenda of the political class, you have a real problem."

"What do you mean?" Graybeard asked, his face creasing up like he'd just heard fighting words.

"I mean if they don't approve of your actions, you will be labeled an extremist. Then they'll haul you off to a re-education camp, brain wash you into their program and then stick you with the bill. Understand?"

Somewhat perturbed, Graybeard finished his beer and left. While the dude ordered another mixed drink and pondered the discussion, the barmaid crept back over for some more talk.

"Those are bad places," she said solemnly, while looking me right in the face. "I wouldn't go there if I were you."

"Huh?" I said, slightly perplexed. "What are you talking about?"

"Those places you want to visit," she clarified. "I was once into those things, but no more. I just read the Gospel, now."

"You mean you know about Bigfoot and the Abominable Snowman?" I asked, testing her depth of knowledge.

"You're wasting your time with that," she sighed.

"What about that lake in Scotland? On Mysterious Worlds, Arthur C. Clark said it might be the ghost of a dinosaur."

"No."

"How about UFOs and Atlantis?" I asked, surely she hadn't completely lost the faith.

"Rubbish!" She declared. "It's all rubbish!"

XXXII

Spiritual Sister

The following morning I met Louise down at the Bistro. She wore faded jeans, a sweater and had sparkling hazel eyes and blond dreadlocks. After a bit of chit-chat we agreed upon an itinerary for the aforementioned sites. Depending on the pace of the day, there was a possibility of visiting the Footprint of God too.

"We'll see," Louise replied. "It's a bit far, yeah."

Michael made an appearance, but was off faster than he arrived.

"I'm three books behind!" He shouted and then peeled out in the driveway.

Loading up in a late model Isuzu 4X4, we ran up the hill and then out onto the N-4 back towards Pretoria.

"So, how did you hear about Michael's work?" Louise asked.

"Every once in awhile I check out a website called Project Camelot," I replied. "About a year and a half ago I heard Michael talking about the "Temples of the African Gods" and the stone ruins all over South Africa. After listening to the interview, I looked up his book on Amazon and bought it."

"That's great," she smiled. "Then you're familiar with his theories."

"Yep, the stone structures were used to channel energy to mine gold tens of thousands of years ago by the Annunaki," I summarized.

"And what do you think," Louise asked earnestly.

"Well," I responded with a bit of hesitation. "I'm not ruling anything out, but if I can speak freely?"

"Sure, go ahead."

"I'm just thinking that if a group of people can build machines that sail across the galaxy, then maybe they have a machine that's used to generate metals. The device might be front loaded with crushed asteroids. Then the debris is bombarded with electro-magnetic energy set at certain frequencies, simulating heat and pressure on particles at the sub-atomic level. The result would be gold, copper, magnesium or rare earth elements generated in days, rather than millions of years."

"That's interesting," Louise replied, and then accelerated to overtake a slower moving vehicle.

"Have you ever wondered if scientists had engineered a device that could harness the power of the Earth's magnetic field?" I asked.

"You mean like a free-energy?"

"Something like that," I said. "But if they have, we'll never see it."

"What do you mean?" Louise replied in a perplexed way.

"Anything that threatens to choke off the money supply isn't going to fly very far."

"You mean the oil companies," Louise confirmed, but in the form of a question.

"For the most part, yeah, but it's not just the fat cats. There are millions of people tied to oil production and consumption. Imagine those people losing their jobs. It would be chaos on a global scale," I said.

"The world shouldn't be like that," Louise added, in a dismayed tone. "We're supposed to be a more holistic society. There's too much anger in the world today."

"You know," I replied. "I always wondered if the establishment was using HAARP to keep everyone in a hostile state."

HAARP, or High Frequency Active Auroral Research Program, is a complex of radio antennas built in Alaska. Officially its function was to study the Ionosphere. However, conspiracy theorists claim it's an electromagnetic weapon that can affect the human mind, manipulate meteorological phenomena and disrupt plate tectonics. In 2014, the US Government announced that HAARP would be dismantled.

"Have you ever heard of Maseru Emoto?" Louise asked.

"Uh-ah, who is he?"

"He's a Japanese scientist who photographs the emotions of water," she said.

Through intense research, Emoto has determined a link between human emotions or speech and the molecular structure of frozen water. Positive thoughts or energy can be captured in the ice. When subjected to violence, the ice forms accordingly. Emoto has a lot of naysayers, but considering the human body is seventy percent water, he may be on to something.

"So, how did you get involved?" Louis asked, meaning what spurned my interest in UFO's, lost cities and strange phenomena.

"It started by catching every episode of "In Search Of" and any UFO or Atlantis special when I was a kid. The stacks of UFO Magazine at my grandparent's house helped too," I laughed.

"Do people agree with you?" Louise asked, her interest somewhat piqued.

"Hah! Now that's a loaded question," I said, and then laughed a bit louder. Through the years, I've learned very few people want to discuss the possibilities of advanced technologies and alien life. Even the most learned people get jumpy or defensive when the subject arises. "Not many."

"So, you're kind of on your own?"

"Yeah, but who cares?" I said, still chuckling. "If the flat-earth believers want to remain intellectually locked down, then so be it."

"Then what are your theories?" Louise continued.

"About?"

"Well, anything…"

"Ok, this is what I think. Say 20,000 years ago there was a scientific race of people who co-existed harmoniously with nature. Meaning, they achieved maximum technical development with very little harm to the environment. Today, we live in a world of scientific materialism where consumer electronics are sold by the millions and environmental impact is an afterthought."

"So, where do you think they were located?" Louise asked, quizzing my position rather than looking for an answer.

"I'd have to say South America for several reasons; first, the Nazca lines. If you look closely there are three different styles. The most identifiable are the geoglyphs of animals, birds and fish. Then there are the spiritual lines that run along and disappear into the distance, but the ones I find most interesting are the geometric shapes that resemble flight decks or air fields."

Louise smiled and then nodded her head in agreement.

"Secondly, in Columbia during the 1950's archaeologists uncovered small gold objects that resembled jet air craft. They show a fuselage, wings and tail fins. Some even have a cockpit, but most have the head of a ferocious animal mounted where the pilot would sit."

"The fabricators of these metallic objects weren't necessarily the builders or operators of prehistoric jet planes. Rather, they were probably common tribesmen (like the jungle Indians of today) who saw them fly overhead and make a loud noise they equated to a jaguar, a caiman or some other tenacious beast. So, they made copies the best way they knew, kind of like the curio dealers near a tourist attraction."

"Yeah, right," Louise agreed. "It makes perfect sense. That's how they tied it to their existence."

"Here's another example," I said. "Take a look at Egypt. Do you really think 10,000 guys on a rope dragged the pyramids at Giza into place? Get lost, man!"

"I know!" Louise said, and then exploded with laughter. "Remember those school books with all the men pushing a huge square rock? So, what do you think happened?"

"To the society?" I replied, confirming the question. "There must have been a cataclysmic event that caused a rapid global catastrophe and knocked them off the grid, the Great Flood or something."

"Yeah, but what do you think caused the flood?"

"Maybe a massive astronomical body passed between the Earth and the Moon and tilted the planet. Have you studied the work of Graham Hancock and Charles Hapgood?" I asked.

In case you're wondering, both researchers are proponents of polar shift. It's a theory stating the earth's axis can change dramatically in a short period of time and generate cataclysmic results on a global scale.

"Of course, but your theory sounds more like Zacharia Sitchin," Louise stated. "Have you read any of his books?"

"Not yet," I replied, but having read a synopsis on "The 12th Planet", some of his work sounded interesting.

Turning off the N-4 Louise angled for higher ground where a trio of ruins staggered down a grassy slope. The rig made a loud metallic rattle (like the under carriage was loose) when she transitioned from paved tarmac to a gravel road. At the top of the hill, she pulled to the side; the first stone circle was just there.

Dense brush had taken root, so, portions of the circle were obscured by vegetation. At ground level it was hard to notice the structure was a massive circle subdivided by compartments. The walls were two meters high in places and stacked from smoothly rounded stones pulled in from a far off river bed.

"What kind of rock is this?" I asked Louise.

"Its black reef shale," she said. "Over half a million of them were used to build this site."

Portions of the stone circle had collapsed outwards, similar to an alluvial flow coming off a mountain. This happens when tall walls built without mortar become unstable, but in another section, someone had pulled down the stones and then stockpiled them for retrieval later.

"This is new," Louise said.

"The place is getting pilfered," I replied, reminiscing on some of the other sites I'd visited.

In violation of all "rules" regarding ancient sites, I climbed up and crept along the top of the walls. One-by-one, the stones clattered against each other and played out musical tones. The organic design and the smooth edges of the stones gave the place an atmosphere of tranquility. Initially, I speculated spiritual brothers from an ancient order had used the place for meditational purposes or transcending the astral plane.

Upon further analysis I began to wonder if the rounded chambers were used for medicinal purposes. Like my scientific reflections in Zimbabwe, you may be scratching your head and wondering what I am alluding to. Well, here it is.

Suppose these spiritualists would go into a trance and begin to chant. The chanting is a vibration. This vibration could be enhanced by the density, shape and surface of the stones as well as the layout of the chamber. As the chanting resonates within the chamber, the sound waves become a medicinal instrument that penetrates the body and cures it from a variety of afflictions and ailments.

Louis held the fort while I set off down the hillside and parted a way through the high grasses, wary that fanged serpents might be ready to strike at my ankles.

Smaller than the first, the second stone circle was more ornate, but lacked the height of the previous ruin. There was a central enclosure from which the rest radiated outward in half circles, kind of like a flower. Atop the rocks was a piece of stone shaped like an implement; it had a long handle and head like a hammer (Louise said stone tools were a common find among the circles). Significant amounts of stone spilled away from the main structure like it had been washed out by heavy rains.

The third circle had the most interesting design; it was in the form of a snake biting its tail (known as an Orobourus). In his book, Tellinger called it a Hindu fertility symbol. In the past, this structure was probably stout, but impressive. Now it was reduced to a much lower profile. The width of the circle's wall was about 1.5 meters and its highest point was probably around 1 meter. The edges of the wall were set in solid stone, but its interior was packed with fill and debris.

Returning to the top of the hill, I found Louise saddled up and ready to move on.

"Hop in," she said. "I want to show you another site."

Continuing on the service road, Louise piloted the rig into the forested hills, plunging down into narrow ravines and then climbing back up to the hill top again. This went on for several repetitions. In one of the troughs, there was an outline of a giant square partially obscured by dense bush. The endeavor was constructed with flat oblong stones of varied width and roughly a meter in length (that's considering the buried portion). They were embedded lengthwise into the ground like planks and wedged tightly together in the form of a low fence or retaining wall. Louise pointed to a couple of stones with rounded shoulders and elongated heads. In general, the planks were slightly reminiscent of the Zimbabwe birds, but lacked any decoration.

Exiting the forest, we came to another complex of stone work overgrown with thick patches of brush. Big animals had bedded down within the ruins and game trails crisscrossed the open areas between the compartments. One of the walls had a square window positioned low to the ground. This site was larger than the previous three combined, but due to the vegetation, it was hard to fully gauge its complexity. However, beyond the rolling landscape an interlinked complex of circles and channels radiated across the nearby hillsides. Having been stripped of its volume and covered with vegetation, the ruins still resembled the base foundation of a long forgotten civilization.

At first, scientists thought the stone circles were nothing more than the remains of Bantu kraals built along the southern migration a couple of hundred years ago. However, when reading

Tellingers' work, it seems the history of the land is layered in several different cultures that sought African gold.

Today, the region is called Mpumalangaland, but before it was known as the Transval and many, many years ago it was called Komatiland. The name Komiti is derived from the Dravidian merchant caste of Southern India. Through the work of Dr. Cyril Mromnik of Cape Town, there is talk that a population of Indians mined gold thousands of years ago. The intermixing of Bushmen, Bantu and Indians gave rise to the MaKomati people (considering Indian Ocean migrations the theory seems plausible). No disrespect to Michael and his research, but the narrative of space brothers loading up their pockets 200,000 years ago seems a bit obtuse. Also, the stone circles are old, but if they were hundreds of thousands of years old wouldn't they be completely buried by now? A safer bet is likely the origins range in the tens of thousands of years.

Here's a little more food for thought: it's easy to think of the stone works as the offshoot of the Grand Zimbabwes. The ruins further north are massive structures woven into the landscape. Though smaller, Tellinger's stone circles are highly repetitive and, at times, broad enough in scope to become the landscape. Knowing this is cause for speculation; a structural engineer from pre-Islamic Arabia ventured upon the stone ruins, conducted examinations and then took what he'd observed north. Once there, he expanded on the dimensions and refined the structures to come up with the first Zimbabwe style. Ultimately the plan of the finest construction, Great Zimbabwe, was taken back to Southern Arabia and then duplicated with slight modifications

Eric P. Mitchell

reflecting the local customs and beliefs of the Sabaen people. Back in Africa, after the originators of the first style departed, the building standards de-evolved as less technically sophisticated peoples sought to copy and reproduce the first style (the yield being Zimbabwe style two through four).

XXXIII

The Stone Man of Mpumalangaland

Heading back east along the R4 we rounded off onto a gravel track and climbed up to Koepshoop, a small hamlet of restaurants, craft shops and guest houses. From there we would advance on a series of Dolerite assemblies that constitute the Calendar site. Dolerite is course grained igneous rock. Louise found a muddy lot and threw it in park. Immediately, we were approached by a lanky black guy in baggy clothes and a faded ball cap. His eyes were glossy and his breath vented off the previous night's beverages.

"This is Enos," Louise said. "He'll guide you around the Calendar site."

"Brother, what's going down?" I said, and then smiled broadly.

Enos returned a grim smile and then nodded sluggishly.

After a quick spin, we landed at the first point, the Stone Man of Mpumalangaland; a column of diorite set vertically into place on a grassy plain with a slight pitch.

"Look closely, you will find the shape of a man," Enos began, tracing the contours of the stone with his hands.

The roughly hewn rock was pitted and spotted by all things that attach themselves to the surface of old stone. In a vague sense it took on the form of human being: a knobby head, thin neck and then a pear-shaped body similar to a stretched bowling pin. Originally, the stone man had come from the main Calendar site, but was moved away in 1992. Two years later it was placed in its current location. At one point, there were two copper plaques affixed to its front. Now, one was missing.

"It is the work of thieves," Enos said, explaining the disappearance.

Next we moved to a clump of trees rooted over a stack of set stones. Enos called it the grave and for good reason, too.

"Five psychics," he said, as his eyes narrowed to watery slits. "All independent of each other, confirmed there are the remains of a 12 foot body buried here. A special camera was brought to this place, too."

"Did it find something good?"

"Yes, a stone structure three meters big," he replied and then stretched his arms outward and emphasized the length and solidity of a heavy object.

Imagine, a twelve foot tall person? It sounds fantastic, but do an Internet search for giant humans and you'll find a lot; a plethora of websites and images regarding the phenomena. A lot of it is over the top or utterly photo shopped; crudely doctored images of massive skeletons at the foot of trawl wielding archaeologists, but there are historical photos showing people of above average height. A prominent spokesman on the subject is Steven Quayle, the author of "Genesis 6 Giants; Master Builders of Prehistoric and Ancient Civilizations". Quayle has been researching the subject for decades and speaks about the topic with a sense of unrestrained urgency. A recent claim is that US forces were attacked by a cave dwelling giant in Afghanistan.

Another authority on the subject is Fritz Zimmerman, whose videos discuss an ancient race of giants that walked the Middle East, Europe and North America. His presentations show diagrams of ancient mounds and henges (a henge is a flat area encircled by a ditch and a berme) still found in the aforementioned places. Zimmerman also discusses Dolemans, curious megalithic constructions consisting of massive slabs of rocks, two or more sides and a flat top (on a side note, there is a book called "Old Stone Monuments' that has a chapter dedicated to Algeria and the Dolmens found there). Probably the most interesting aspect of Zimmerman's work is a series of images depicting oversized skulls that have been found all over the world.

Digging further online, you'll also find a chart depicting a collection of skeletons that have "been documented in the human record". The diagram begins with a 6 foot example and then meanders a bit between 8.5 and 15 foot specimens. After leaping to 19.5 feet, the skeletons surpass 25 and then culminate at a

36 foot tall beast. Below each example is a brief description like "present day man", "S/E Turkey 1950's", and "1456 AD France, beside river".

Entitled "Giants in South Africa", Michael Tellinger also has a video interview with a professor at his Alma Matter, Witts University. In preparation for the meeting, the professor has set aside the remnants of a human femur. Dull and tarnished, the specimen is the upper half, where the ball joint fits into the hip bone. The Professor indicates the remains were discovered in the 1960s by miners in the Otavi Mountains of Northern Namibia.

"It's anatomically correct," he acknowledges, and then places the specimen next to a modern day bone for comparison. The artifact is more than twice the size of its contemporary. You have to wonder, did its owner stand between 10-12 feet tall? If so, this would classify it as a giant. Because of its mineralized state, the femur cannot be carbon dated. However, the professor speculates the bone is roughly 100,000 years old.

That explains the lower end of the chart. However, the higher end of the spectrum seems absolutely fantastic, or does it? In an area called Mpuluzi, near the border with Swaziland, you can see human spoor of staggering proportions. Slightly crumpled up at the toes like the giant had been moving quickly across a flat surface, the "Footprint of God" as it's known, is embedded vertically in an outcropping of rough granite (plate tectonics have jostled it a bit). It's estimated to be 200 million years old. At four feet in length the beast that left his track would stand up at around 24 feet tall, well within the dimensions of the previously mentioned document.

Although it seems fantastic, the archaeological record is clear. There is a lost race of people considerably taller than contemporary man. After reviewing the more credible information, you're left wondering, what forces gave mankind such amazing stature. Was it a flood of cosmic radiation or was there a hotter climate and greater air pressure during prehistoric times?

Further along we came to a field of rocks that resembled a micro version of Carnac, the field of megalithic stones in France. Half pint bobble heads at semi-regular intervals were lined up in a several rows. Waylaid, the largest specimens lay in the mud-like abandoned corpses, but amongst the debris there was a stone of special note.

"Here we begin the ceremonial path to the Calendar site," Enos stated, and then gestured towards a slab of rock stretched low across the ground. "This is the South African Sphinx."

Although heavily weathered, the contoured rock had a pronounced head, elongated body and rounded hind quarters. Its length was equivalent to a man with average height and resembled a lion on its haunches in the grass, just like the icon at Giza.

XXXIV

The End

In some regards Adam's Calendar is a relatively new site on the archaeology scene. Having endured a bit of obscurity, the ruins were brought to mainstream attention by Tellinger after a friend, Johan Heine, spotted the site from the air. As Heine made repeated passes over the Barberton Escarpment in a helicopter, he noticed a peculiar arrangement of megalithic stones. Alerting Michael to the discovery, the two men ventured to the site and began their research. A coffee table book titled "Adam's

Calendar" is the culmination of their efforts. It's loaded with photographs of the monolithic rocks at every conceivable angle. Some of the best shots are of the early morning sun rising in line with the site's most prominent feature, the calendar stones.

The exact time of construction is unclear, but through astronomic research, a scientist has determined that the site can be dated in increments of 25,000 years. Tellinger claims the site was originally aligned with the constellation Orion, but paleo-astronomy wasn't the only means of dating. As with the tree clump, a handful of psychics made their assessment too. Through clairvoyance they determined Adam's Calendar was 75,000 to 80,000 years old, matching the date range of the paleo-astronomer. Tellinger goes on to state that the psychics also claim the stones are the work of the Sumerian deity, Enki.

Most of the standing stones are squat and have a low profile. With exception to the two calendar stones, any specimen of significance has been toppled over and lay embedded in the soil. At two meters plus, they are megalithic in the truest sense of the word. Broad, long and flat, some take on male and feminine forms (Adam and Eve?). Possibly the most thought provoking example is a massive shank with a curved top and notch cut out giving it a hawk like beak; once again, the birds!

Standing well over two meters high, the Calendar stones are by far the largest specimens, but they haven't fared so well. Both are listing dangerously and on the verge of capsizing. Though the monoliths have suffered fracturing and are covered with a mosaic of lichens (fungus based organisms that grow in crusty leaf like patches), the detailed work of ancient craftsman are still visible.

As Enos leaned over one of the stones a dark shadow stretched across the weathered rock reducing the sun's reflection.

"Look here," he instructed, and then ran his hand over the rough stone surface and pointed to the faint ribbing worked into the rock. "These are the calendar lines that correspond with shadows from the other main stone."

"So, what does it mean?" I asked.

"The main stones are vibration plates," he said. "And this site is for initiation rites, energy channeling and meditation ceremonies."

Heavy grasses and a general state of disarray make for a confusing site. However, on page 122 in the book "Adam's Calendar" an overhead diagram of the stones is combined with lines depicting the equinox and both the winter and spring solstice. The solstice is the astronomical event when the sun reaches its highest or lowest position in regards to the equator. This event happens twice a year; once in the northern hemisphere and once in the southern hemisphere. The equinox is another celestial event that occurs when the light and dark hours of the day are equal; on March 20 and September 22. A second illustration depicts Adam's Calendar in near longitudinal alignment with Great Zimbabwe and the Pyramids at Giza.

Of all the sites I'd visited since starting out in Ethiopia, Adam's Calendar looked the oldest of them all. They are the remains of something very ancient, but what, exactly, is unclear. However, being they bear a slight resemblance to the likes of Stonehenge, though on a much smaller scale, the concept of celestial or solar observations may be an accurate assessment.

As a closing observation, the prominence of bird representations should be considered as well. Slightly similar, the Stone Circle fowl resemble the Zimbabwe flock, without the ornamentation. A relation to ancient Egypt is plausible, but what if they were brought to southern Africa by a lost race from the other side of the Indian Ocean? An exceptionally motivated adventurer might travel to Mayalasia or Indonesia, organize a small team of locals and then wade into the Jungles searching for such artifacts.

Strolling over to the edge of the escarpment, I gazed down into the Barberton Impact Crater. The depression was full of lush green vegetation and spotted by all types of buildings. Off in the distance two cone shaped hills broke the plain of the crater floor.

"What's going on out there?" I said, directing the question at Enos.

"In the valley below?" He replied. "Those are three pyramids centered in the depression. Two are visible and a smaller one is buried to the right as we face them. They are seventy meters in height. When standing at the top all types of electronics behave poorly."

"Like how?"

"You see, the compass can just spin," he said, and then whirled his finger in a circle. "Laptops turn off all by themselves and small GPS will give inaccurate readings."

"Then let's go down there," I said, thinking of taking the summit.

"They're on private property," Louise said.

"So what!" I replied, in a jocular way. "We can fix bayonets and take the objective!"

Louise shook her head and laughed, "You really are an adventurer."

"And what about the Footprint of God?" Louise and I still had a tentative plan to visit, or did we?

"There's not enough time," she said. "It's getting to be late afternoon."

Unsatisfied with her answer, I retrieved the last C-note from my bag of sensitive items and pulled the birdie trick once again.

"Look, a hundred bucks," I pleaded, and then flapped the bill up and down. "Right here, see it?"

"Sorry, Eric," she smiled.

Standing at the edge of the escarpment, I gazed back out into the crater and reflected back on the last few months. Walking through Ethiopia or jumping on a bus in Tanzania seemed like just yesterday. In flash, the faces of Gelila, the antiquities specialist, Ateino, good ole Maps, Brother James, and Thomas and Loice went through my mind. Images of all the places I visited followed; Yeha Temple, the Cave of Skulls, boating to Sanje ya Kati and the Outpost. I was going to miss the Foot Print of God and I'd skipped some ruins in Mozambique, but I'd seen the best that East and Southern Africa had to offer. With my visa expiring in less than two days and my cash position hovering just above ground zero, my journey had ended, not fully complete, but over for the time being. Soon, I'd be on that big bird in the sky soaring back home.

That said there is still a task at hand for any guerilla archaeologist who's made it this far into the essay. Imagine you've completed a reconnaissance via Google Earth, landed in country and organized your team (you'll need at least one partner to help carry the tools). Skirting across the fields in the wee hours of the night, you hack away the brush and tunnel a way to the top of one of the "pyramids". There you can find a suitable place to dig a trench. First, chop through the vegetation and then scrap away the overburden. As dawn slowly radiates the horizon you finally hit stone. Is it just an out cropping of rock or is it an archaeological discovery that will rock the foundations of today's civilization. There's only one way to find out. So, what are you waiting for? Get going!

Book List

Ethiopia

Ancient Churches of Ethiopia, 2009. David W. Phillipson
Ethiopia: the Unknown Land, 2002. Stuart Munro-Hay
The Sacred City of the Ethiopians, 1896. J. Theodore Bent
The Sign and the Seal, 1992. Graham Hancock

Kenya/Tanzania

Lost Cities & Ancient Mysteries of Africa & Arabia, 1989. David Hatcher Childress
The Lost Cities of Africa, 1959. Basil Davidson
Men and Monuments of the East African Coast, 1966. James S. Kirkman

Zimbabwe

The Ancient Ruins of Rhodesia, 1904. Richard Nicklin Hall and W.G. Neal
The Lost City of Solomon & Sheba; an African Mystery, 2003. Robin Brown-Lowe
The Origin of the Zimbabwe Civilization, 1972. R. Gayre of Gayre
Medaeval Rhodesia, 1906. David Randell-Maciver
Monomotapa (Rhodesia), 1896. Alexander Wilmot

South Africa

Adam's Calendar, 2008. Johan Heine and Michael Tellinger

Disclosure, 2001. Steven M. Greer M.D.

Temple of the African Gods, 2010. Michael Tellinger and Johan Heine

Unsolved Mysteries of Southern Africa, 1994. Rob Marsh

Bag of Sensitive Items

Passport.
Stack of crisp 100 Dollar Bills.
Two books of Traveler's Checks.
Laptop.
Digital Camera.
Variety of Electrical Adapters.
One Field Kit.
One 1 liter bottle of Water.
Two 500 milli-liter bottles of Coca-cola.
One Roll Tango Papa.

Made in the USA
Las Vegas, NV
05 November 2021